Quod scriptura, non iubet vetat

The Latin translates, "What is not commanded in scripture, is forbidden:'

On the Cover: Baptists rejoice to hold in common with other evangelicals the main principles of the orthodox Christian faith. However, there are points of difference and these differences are significant. In fact, because these differences arise out of God's revealed will, they are of vital importance. Hence, the barriers of separation between Baptists and others can hardly be considered a trifling matter. To suppose that Baptists are kept apart solely by their views on Baptism or the Lord's Supper is a regrettable misunderstanding. Baptists hold views which distinguish them from Catholics, Congregationalists, Episcopalians, Lutherans, Methodists, Pentecostals, and Presbyterians, and the differences are so great as not only to justify, but to demand, the separate denominational existence of Baptists. Some people think Baptists ought not teach and emphasize their differences but as E.J. Forrester stated in 1893, "Any denomination that has views which justify its separate existence, is bound to promulgate those views. If those views are of sufficient importance to justify a separate existence, they are important enough to create a duty for their promulgation ... the very same reasons which justify the separate existence of any denomination make it the duty of that denomination to teach the distinctive doctrines upon which its separate existence rests." If Baptists have a right to a separate denominational life, it is their duty to propagate their distinctive principles, without which their separate life cannot be justified or maintained.

Many among today's professing Baptists have an agenda to revise the Baptist distinctives and redefine what it means to be a Baptist. Others don't understand why it even matters. The books being reproduced in the *Baptist Distinctives Series* are republished in order that Baptists from the past may state, explain and defend the primary Baptist distinctives as they understood them. It is hoped that this Series will provide a more thorough historical perspective on what it means to be distinctively Baptist.

The Lord Jesus Christ asked, *"And why call ye me, Lord, Lord, and do not the things which I say?"* (Luke 6:46). The immediate context surrounding this question explains what it means to be a true disciple of Christ. Addressing the same issue, Christ's question is meant to show that a confession of discipleship to the Lord Jesus Christ is inconsistent and untrue if it is not accompanied with a corresponding submission to His authoritative commands. Christ's question teaches us that a true recognition of His authority as Lord inevitably includes a submission to the authority of His Word. Hence, with this question Christ has made it forever impossible to separate His authority as King from the authority of His Word. These two principles—the authority of Christ as King and the authority of His Word—are the two most fundamental Baptist distinctives. The first gives rise to the second and out of these two all the other Baptist distinctives emanate. As F.M. Iams wrote in 1894, "Loyalty to Christ as King, manifesting itself in a constant and unswerving obedience to His will as revealed in His written Word, is the real source of all the Baptist distinctives:' In the search for the *primary* Baptist distinctive many have settled on the Lordship of Christ as the most basic distinctive. Strangely, in doing this, some have attempted to separate Christ's Lordship from the authority of Scripture, as if you could embrace Christ's authority without submitting to what He commanded. However, while Christ's Lordship and Kingly authority can be isolated and considered essentially for discussion's sake, we see from Christ's own words in Luke 6:46 that His Lordship is really inseparable from His Word and, with regard to real Christian discipleship, there can be no practical submission to the one without a practical submission to the other.

In the symbol above the Kingly Crown and the Open Bible represent the inseparable truths of Christ's Kingly and Biblical authority. The Crown and Bible graphics are supplemented by three Bible verses (Ecclesiastes 8:4, Matthew 28:18-20, and Luke 6:46) that reiterate and reinforce the inextricable connection between the authority of Christ as King and the authority of His Word. The truths symbolized by these components are further emphasized by the Latin quotation - *quod scriptura, non iubet vetat*— *i.e.,* "What is not commanded in scripture, is forbidden:' This Latin quote has been considered historically as a summary statement of the regulative principle of Scripture. Together these various symbolic components converge to exhibit the two most foundational Baptist Distinctives out of which all the other Baptist Distinctives arise. Consequently, we have chosen this composite symbol as a logo to represent the primary truths set forth in the *Baptist Distinctives Series.*

Behind the Scenes

BEHIND THE SCENES:

SKETCHES FROM REAL LIFE.

BY F. M. IAMS

"Prove all things; hold fast that which is good."—I Thess. v. 21.

With a Biographical Sketch of the Author by John Franklin Jones

LOUISVILLE, KY:
BAPTIST BOOK CONCERN.
1894.

The Baptist Standard Bearer, Inc.
NUMBER ONE IRON OAKS DRIVE • PARIS, ARKANSAS 72855

Thou hast given a *standard* to them that fear thee;
that it may be displayed because of the truth.
– Psalm 60:4

Reprinted 2006

by

THE BAPTIST STANDARD BEARER, INC.
No. 1 Iron Oaks Drive
Paris, Arkansas 72855
(479) 963-3831

THE WALDENSIAN EMBLEM
lux lucet in tenebris
"The Light Shineth in the Darkness"

ISBN# 1579786367

PREFACE TO THE TENTH EDITION.

Having occasion to issue the tenth edition of "Behind the Scenes," the publisher takes occasion to say that it has been one of the most successful books offered to the Christian public. It has been received with marked favor in all parts of the country, and where it is best known the sales are largest. It has been the means of convincing a large number of pedobaptists, among them several ministers of the gospel, of the validity of the Baptist position, and it is still going on its way, confirming the souls of the faithful and winning others to the truth.

The author, who was for many years a highly esteemed pastor of Baptist churches, recently laid down the cross that he might take the crown.

CINCINNATI, *December*, 1892.

AUTHOR'S PREFACE.

THESE sketches are not drafts upon the imagination. They are simple narratives of actual incidents in the experience of the writer together with such reflections and arguments as seemed to him pertinent and appropriate. There is in them no attempt at fine writing. If the style is plain, compact and earnest, so was the somewhat unique experience that gave it birth. A man who has walked amid the flames of a furnace may be excused, perhaps, if his account of the adventure lacks the genial aimlessness of an amusing fiction.

But however strong the desire to make the truth of God evident to the reader of these pages, the author is conscious of none other than the kindest feelings toward those whose views and practices he is obliged to condemn. He has written, not to denounce nor to offend, but to convince, and if possible, to win very dear brethren. His only desire is to induce Christian brethren to walk together in that unity so delightful and so enduring; the unity of obedience to Christ as King. This is the only unity of any real value. The unity of indifference, now so popular in many quarters, is not born of a consuming love of the truth—nor does it tend to promote the

AUTHOR'S PREFACE.

truth. "The wisdom that is from above is first pure, then peaceable" — peaceable tnrough the truth, not at the expense of truth. Such wisdom is from God, enthrones God, honors him above all else, and lifts the soul into the serene atmosphere of divine peace.

That these pages are free from faults and blemishes the author dare not hope. That they treat the subject exhaustively he does not claim. But that they treat it with fairness and Christian candor he feels quite assured.

In the confident hope that they will prove helpful to earnest, inquiring minds, and that God will graciously use them to promote the "truth as it is in Jesus," I send them forth, praying that the blessing of God may rest upon every reader.

F. M. IAMS.

CONTENTS.

		PAGE.
No. 1.	"Only a Dedication,"	7
No. 2.	"Vot's de Good of It?"	18
No. 3.	"Let Me Alone,"	32
No. 4.	Lint on the Nib,	45
No. 5.	"Valid Baptism,"	59
No. 6.	My Resolution,	73
No. 7.	A Presbyterian Prophecy,	86
No. 8.	Those German Scholars,	103
No. 9.	"A Grand Book,"	116
No. 10.	Letting Providence Decide,	131
No. 11.	A Puzzled Preacher,	144
No. 12.	"What can you Plead?"	158
No. 13.	"I Never Could Understand,"	191
No. 14.	The Final Test,	214

BEHIND THE SCENES.

NUMBER I.

" It's only a Dedication."

In the autumn of 185– I accepted the unanimous call of the Congregational Church in the village of T——. I was then only a licentiate, but the next spring, after due examination by a Council called by the church, I was solemnly ordained to the full work of the gospel ministry. I entered upon the sacred duties of the holy calling, not without many misgivings respecting my ability to discharge them properly, and yet with a joyous and earnest consecration of heart, intellect and life to the great work.

A son of the grand old University of B——, I naturally carried with me into the sacred desk something of the vigorous, indomitable spirit of my dear old *Alma Mater*. I was an earnest student of books rather than of men, and of ideas rather than books. Nor did this produce a drift of thought in the direction of the visionary, but rather the reverse. My intense desire to do good anchored me to the practical, while my profound reverence for Bible truth made me an earnest student of doctrines. As the result, my preaching was at once plain, direct, argumentative and practical. My dear people were constantly drawn closer to me, and I heartily reciprocated their confidence and affection, and we soon became almost glued, as it were, into one harmonious, inseparable body.

We were enthusiastic Congregationalists. Hopkins, Bellamy and Dwight were our oracles, and Plymouth Rock, once pressed by the sacred feet of the immaculate old Puritans, was our beloved blarney-stone, and I suppose we, half unconsciously, pitied those poor, unfortunate churches which have no Plymouth Rock to fall back upon, nor any May Flower to boast of.

From the first I had frequent occasion to baptize infants, and I always did it properly, cheerfully and reverently, and to the edification of all concerned in it.

Thus matters wore a pleasant aspect, and as time moved on, life seemed one long, cloudless, balmy June day, laden with the aroma of the sweetest flowers, and enlivened with inspiring harmonies.

But there came a change. In the progress of my Bible study I soon found myself disturbed by grave doubts respecting the scripturalness of infant baptism. I saw clearly that the baptism of believers was enjoined by our Lord, and that the practice of the apostles accorded with that injunction.

But that Christ required the baptism of babes, or that the apostles practiced such baptism, was not so clear. I tried to put away my doubts, and sometimes I succeeded for a short time, but they would not stay put away. Often, when I least expected it, they would return in full force, and give me no little trouble. At length I began to look into our usual defenses of the practice a little more closely, and I was at once surprised, and not a little perplexed, at the evident and numerous weaknesses in them. This greatly increased my gathering doubts; and, as if to add to my difficulties—though she knew nothing of them—a good sister presented her young child for baptism. I was in a most painful dilemma. I could not well refuse to baptize the babe—and yet I did not dare to baptize it. By refusing to baptize it I would probably offend and grieve the entire church; but on the other hand, by baptizing it I might offend and grieve my Master, the great Head of the Church. For a few moments I did not know what to do; there seemed to be no way out of the difficulty. But presently a happy thought came to my relief. I told the mother of the child privately that I had lately come to have some doubts about infant baptism, and that I desired her to delay the baptism of her babe until the next communion season (a period of two months), that I might have time to examine the matter more fully. I also requested her to say nothing about my doubts to any one. These requests she readily granted, and the baptism of the babe was postponed.

During the next two months I studied infant baptism with great diligence, but with very little success. I could not quite make up my mind either way, and as the next communion season was at hand, I was obliged to ask that sister for another postponement of two months. This she granted, and I went on with the investigation. But I found my doubts increasing rapidly, and at the next communion I told her I did not dare baptize her babe then, and I desired another postponement, which she readily granted. Continuing my examination of the subject, I now became fully convinced, to my great dismay, that infant baptism has no warrant in the Word of God. But what could I do? If I gave up infant baptism, I must also give up the work of the ministry, to which I firmly believed God had called me, or I must leave my people and become a Baptist. I could not leave the ministry. I must continue to preach the gospel, for that duty was very clear and very urgent. But if I rejected infant baptism, I could not remain a Congregational minister. For, although we boasted our liberality, and allowed the greatest diversity of views among our members, we were very exacting with our ministers. No man could long be a minister among us, if he was known to reject infant baptism or sprinkling. If I gave up infant baptism, therefore, I must leave my church and go to the Baptists. But I could not do that, for, in my opinion, they were a narrow, bigoted people at the best, and I hated their horrible close communion. I was now in very great distress. What to do I did not know.

Three things were becoming very clear to me: I could not continue the practice of infant baptism, for it was not scriptural; rejecting it, I could not remain in the ministry in a Congregational Church. In any event, I could not be a Baptist. It was also evident that I must soon do something decisive. I had secured another postponement of the baptism of that babe, and if he was ever to have the benefit of *infant* baptism, he must be baptized soon.

I now remembered having heard infant baptism defended as a pious act of dedication—an act in which the parents and the church unitedly presented the child to God, covenanting to bring him up in the nurture and admonition of the Lord. This arrested my attention and impressed me favorably. In common with my brethren, I had already come to look upon adult baptism as chiefly a solemn self-dedication of the baptized one to the service of God. I had been taught that this dedication was indeed the only essential thing in baptism. This put the whole question before me in a new light. It no longer appeared so much a question of baptism as a pious act of dedication. I knew that, practically, all pedobaptists treat infant baptism as a nullity, if it be not in more mature years fully adopted and confirmed as his own act, by the one to whom it has been administered. And here, evidently, was the true explanation of that fact. They regarded the infant baptism not as a baptism, but as a dedication—*to become a baptism only when accepted as such by the grown-up child.* This is a beautiful and flexible arrangement. I apply the water to the child in the name of the Trinity; yet I do not baptize it, but only dedicate it. In all true baptism there must be the intelligent assent of the subject. But the infant does not and can not give such assent; and therefore, while he is dedicated to God in the solemn formula of baptism, he is not baptized. An essential element—his own assent —is lacking. When, in after years, he gives that assent, the church will for the first time treat him as really baptized. Should he refuse such assent, the church would refuse to regard him as baptized.

It is plain, then, that I do not baptize him. I only dedicate him, and he afterward takes that dedication and makes it a baptism. *The dedication is my act, and the baptism is his act.* If the dedication is proper I am all right, and if the baptism is wrong it is his fault.

That this conclusion is correct must be conceded by every pedobaptist. For the ceremony of confirmation is the concluding act of infant baptism—that act which completes it and makes it baptism—if anything does. Until it receives confirmation, the child is treated by the church as unbaptized. The Lord's Supper and all other church privileges are denied it, but at and after confirmation they are at once accorded to it. The only possible defense the church can set up for her conduct in the matter is, that the confirmation completes the baptism—makes it valid—and thus entitles the child to all the privileges of a baptized person. Either the child was baptized by, or in confirmation, or, having been baptized before, it was basely and systematically robbed of its most sacred religious rights by the church. The truth is, that confirmation is virtually a confession that an intelligent personal assent is an indispensable element of baptism. It is true this confession overturns infant baptism, by recognizing an element in baptism which is impossible to all infants. But the confession is a true and healthy one for all that.

Here I found a door of hope. I could not baptize an infant; but I could and would dedicate it; and if, in after years, the infant chose to convert the dedication into a baptism, that would not be my fault. Accordingly at our next communion service, I told my church, that I could no longer consent to baptize infants, but that I was entirely willing to dedicate them to God. After stating my new views briefly, I told the church that, if they could agree with me to regard the service not as a baptism, but simply as a dedication, we could still go on together; but if not, we must separate. I invited any one who might desire to express dissent to do so at once. I paused, but no one spoke a single word. Then, accepting their silence as a token of unanimous assent to my plan, I proceeded to dedicate that long postponed babe, using the old baptismal service—water, words, and all—not omitting a single thing. I said, "I baptize thee," etc., all the time meaning, I dedicate thee. This was certainly a very singular proceeding in many respects, and I have often wondered at it myself, but I saw nothing improper in it at that time. Indeed, I felt very devout and happy, and my people seemed to feel so too—which only indicates how unsafe it is to take our feelings as a criterion of duty.

I am perfectly sure, now, that I acted conscientiously in the whole matter; but the trouble was with my conscience. It was honest and active, but it was not enlightened. I verily believed that I was doing God service, and I regarded myself as really a person of some considerable ability and shrewdness, since I had got out of such an exceedingly tight spot in a way so ingenious and creditable. Still, as I was not without an occasional fear lest, after all, it might not be exactly the right thing, I refrained from boasting, contenting myself with a little private rejoicing, that, after all, I could remain with my dear people. And so for some years I went on dedicating the babes, often wincing not a little at the stormy doubts which persisted in gathering about me, more and more as time advanced, and which did not cease their assaults until I ceased to say, "It's only a dedication."

Indeed, I felt very devout and happy, and my people seemed to feel so too—which only indicates how unsafe it is to take our feelings as a criterion of duty.

And yet our feelings are not to be ignored or despised. They have their legitimate uses—uses beautiful and beneficent. They are the "juices of life," if the expression may be permitted, converting otherwise dry and dreary wastes into fertile fields, full of springing buds and ripening fruits. They are the chief motive power in multitudes of human hearts and lives, and, it may be, an inseparable factor in all right moral action.

But our feelings, while they are grand servants, helping us in a thousand ways, are miserable guides.

The truth is, they have no eyes—they are blind—and unaided by the mind, they are quite as apt to go in a wrong direction as in the way of right. If one has a mistaken idea of duty, and lives up to that idea, he will feel happy over it until he discovers his mistake. And if that man makes feeling his test of duty and of right, he may go on many years in positive wrong-doing without knowing it; or in the utter and even contemptuous neglect of urgent duty without so much as once suspecting it.

Nor is it enough that we be conscientious. We may be very conscientious, and, at the same time, be very far from right. The treacherous Thug is conscientious, religiously so, in his foul work of assassination. Saul of Tarsus was a conscientious persecutor of the Church of God. Doubtless, the grim judges of the Inquisition were conscientious. It is not enough to say, "I have the approval of my conscience" in doing this or that. The Word of God is the supreme rule of right, and we are safe only when feeling and conscience are conformed to that divine rule.

I am perfectly sure, now, that I acted conscientiously in the whole matter; but the trouble was with my conscience.

2

NUMBER II.

"To pe sure you can; and if you can't, vot's de good of it?"

ONE day, while pastor of the church in the village of T——, I was walking in the country, at a distance of several miles from home. As I was passing a plain, neat farm-house, the door opened and a woman came out and hailed me. She was the farmer's wife, a tidy German woman, whom I had met not long before at a country wedding.

Coming toward the gate, she said: "Pees you de minister at T——?" I confessed that I was. Then she asked anxiously, "Does you paptize papies?" I acknowledged that I was in the habit of doing so. Then she came to business at once in these words: "Vell, den, I vants you to come right in, and paptize my dree leetle vuns." I told her how glad I would be to comply with her request, were it proper to do so. I then carefully explained the nature of the ceremony; that it was a covenant between the parents of the children and the church, in which they, together, gave the children to the Lord, and agreed to train them up "in the nurture and admonition of the Lord;" whence it was necessary that it should be observed in the presence of the church, and that at least one of the parents should be a member of the church. I invited her to bring her children to our meeting in the village, to unite with the church herself, and then to have her little ones baptized.

I was astonished at the effect of my quiet matter-of-fact words. "Ah, no," she cried, "it pees a long vay to de town, and ve got no team. It pees a long time pefore ve can come to de town; and maype de poor leetle tings die, mit no paptism, an den dey perish shoost like de peasts of the field; dey got no soul, no immortality, no eternal life, 'cause dey not paptized!"

It was a cry of anguish. All her mother heart seemed compressed into her poor broken words. Her voice was tremulous with feeling, and every word seemed drenched in tears.

Evidently she was terribly in earnest, and regarded the baptism of her children as a matter of the highest moment, involving their eternal destiny. It was a fearful revelation to me. I had read much about such distorted views of baptism, but they had always seemed to me so exaggerated and impossible that I had regarded them rather as the wild vagaries of crack-brained theorists, than as the actual convictions of men and women in real life. But here I was suddenly confronted by an earnest, misguided mother, pleading for baptism at my hands, to save her own dear babes from eternal death. Was ever any pagan superstition worse than that? I was amazed, shocked, and, for a few moments, thoroughly upset. As soon as I could rally my bewildered wits, I tried to convince her that she greatly overestimated baptism; that it had no such saving virtue, and that her children would not be lost for want of it, even if they should die without it. But the training and prejudices of a lifetime were not to be overcome in an hour. I could make no impression upon her citadel of superstition. At length, in very desperation, I cried out: "Do you really think I can give your children immortality, eternal life, by putting a little water on them?"

Her answer came swift, strong, and utterly confounding to all half-way pedobaptists—"To pe sure you can; and if you can't, vots de good of it?"

Finding that I could not change her views of the efficacy of baptism, I declined to baptize her little ones under any circumstances.

I went home in a brown study, her bold, incisive

and rigidly logical question—"*Vot's de good of it?*"—ringing in my ears at a fearful rate. And, day after day, that same question—"*Vot's de good of it?*"—would pop up everywhere, like some irrepressible imp, meeting me at every turn—grinning at me from every nook and cranny—mocking at me in all possible ways—but ever growing bolder and more urgent and more imperious. I could neither escape it, nor banish it, nor answer it.

At length I reluctantly confessed myself vanquished, and gave up the practice of infant baptism—a practice which God has not enjoined—a practice which no man can defend, except by the false pretense that there is in it some hidden, saving efficacy—some secret power to save the soul. "Vot's de good of it?" sure enough. Who can tell? What is the good of it? What has it ever done? What of blessing has it ever conferred on the church, the world or the family? How has it ever benefited one of its unconscious subjects? It has done evil enough—and the evil it has done is evident enough—but what good has it ever done? Ask history, and she will point to the darkest of her many blood-stained pages, and tell you these are the records of its evil deeds. It brought the world into the church, unregenerate, godless, impenitent. It introduced into the church the men who invented the Papacy, the men who contrived its machinery, the men who fostered its corruptions, the men whose unholy ambitions developed its fearful power.

It is not the child but the mother of the Papacy. It existed before the Papacy, and its existence made the Papacy possible. It is the mother and conservator of every State Church on earth. It is the one thing indispensable to every State Church. It keeps alive all State Churches to-day, with all their festering corruptions. Take it away, and Romanism would die in a single generation. Abolish it, and you abolish Episcopacy in England and Lutheranism in Germany. Abolish it, and you make persecution for religious opinions forever impossible among the professed disciples of Christ. Infant baptism and persecution were absolutely inseparable for more than thirteen hundred years. Only such churches as cherished infant baptism have been guilty of the great sin of persecution. And of all those churches only one, the Methodist, can rise up and truthfully say, we have never persecuted. That Church "retains" infant baptism, but so carelessly and illogically, that it has never had its legitimate influence on her spirit and life. From the first, Methodism, with a happy inconsistency, has practically ignored infant baptism, while retaining it, insisting on a converted membership in all her classes, thus keeping herself, in a large measure, free from its debasing influences.

The evil that infant baptism has done is written in letters of blood on almost every page of the history of christendom, and on myriads of wronged human hearts; but the good that it has done is written—where? Alas, echo answers always and only—where? Go through the world and search it out; find it if you can; measure it soberly by the divine Word; weigh it in the scales of divine truth, and then publish it to the ends of the earth.

But if you find no good, but only evil, and that continually; if you find many thousands, like that poor German mother, depending upon infant baptism to save their children; if you find scores of thousands trusting in their own baptism in infancy to save them; if you find multitudes thus blinded groping in the darkness, and kept away from Christ by it; if you find it the chief prop of Romanism, of all State Churches, of all ecclesiastical usurpations, tyrannies, persecutions and corruptions—then be assured it is not of God, but of antichrist, and that no man can be innocent in the sight of Jehovah who contributes by his influence to perpetuate it.

"*Vot's de good of it?*" Suppose you go through this land proposing this same question in every church where infant baptism is practiced, and note the astonishing variety of replies.

One tells you that it is a testimony to the goodness of human nature, that it certifies the holiness of infancy, and assures us that the evil within us is outweighed and overborne by the good; but another tells you that it is a solemn witness to our depravity, assuming it to be so great that even unconscious babes imperatively need the washing of regeneration in the baptismal laver, to put away the corruption of original sin. You repeat the question, and you are told by one that the baptism is a recognition of the membership of the babe in the Church of Christ, by virtue of its Christian parentage; while another gravely assures you that the baptism makes it a member of the Church of Christ, into which, he tells you, no one, not even the children of Christian parents, can enter without being baptized; while still another informs you that the baptized babe is not in the church at all.

You move on, a little confused, and repeat

the inquiry, and one hastens to reply that the baptism washes away original sin; another that it regenerates the child, and makes him a member of Christ's kingdom, a subject of his grace, and an heir of heaven; while another assures you that it has no effect whatever upon the babe, but expends all its force for good upon the parents and the church.

This staggers you somewhat, but again you move on, in a dazed sort of way, and reverently ask: "*Vot's the good of it?*" A solemn voice replies, "It secures to the babe all the benefits of the covenant of grace;" but another voice, equally solemn, assures you that it is not so, that it has nothing to do with any sort of covenant, gracious or otherwise, but that it is a divine institution, "in the same sense that an ox-yoke is;" but another voice, equally solemn, interrupts, informing you that there is neither covenant nor ox-yoke about it, but an æsthetic and sentimental beauty, very pleasing to the proud and happy parents.

This sunflower theology may puzzle you a little, but go on and press your problem, and other voices will greet you with replies far harder to digest. One tells you that every babe that dies unbaptized goes down into the pit; that no human being, young or old, dying without baptism, can be saved. Another assures you that he rejects with loathing a doctrine so horrible; but that by baptism the infant is made a partaker of the "covenanted mercies of God," so that his salvation is, in a manner, thereby assured.

Thus the defense of infant baptism is a theological "Tower of Babel," a veritable "confusion of tongues," imperiling the peace and sanity of every honest inquirer after the truth. Men of views the most contradictory practice this unscriptural rite in search of benefits to the last degree imaginary, and for reasons the most antagonistic and irreconcilable.

If the subject were not so grave, it would be very amusing to witness the deliberations of a great convention of learned and pious pedobaptist divines, engaged in the awful task of framing a respectable and official reply to this little, rustic-looking, but dangerous and monitor-like problem, "*Vot's the good of it?*"

Long before they could agree upon a definite answer, there would be such a "Babel of tongues" among them that the convention would explode in "holy wrath," while the uncircumcised spectator would also explode, but in guileless merriment.

Just imagine such a convention in session, engaged in the mighty deliberation. Here are

Catholic and Episcopalian, Lutheran and Presbyterian, Reformed and Congregational and Methodist, conferring together about the benefits of a practice common to all of them.

They are all ardent but discordant devotees of infant baptism. The reverend chairman states the question in words so brief, they might be defined the soul of wit:

"My brethren—Doubtless we all love infant baptism dearly; it is such a blessing to the little dears. And we all practice it most reverently, as is fitting in men so reverend. But we have fallen on evil times. There are uneasy souls abroad who question its utility, and they meet us at every turn with questions hard to answer. Pressed by them on all sides, we have met in this great and wise convention to discuss the matter freely, and, if possible, to frame a conclusive and official answer to this annoying problem, 'Vot's de good of it? Brethren, proceed."

"Vot's de good of it?" cries the Catholic priest. "Why, sir, it is a saving sacrament. It confers salvation, and without it, the dying babe is certainly lost. If unbaptized, it is only heathen, and its dead body can not have interment in a Catholic burying-ground, nor its soul admission into heaven. This is the doctrine of Holy Church."

"Ah," says the Episcopalian, "you are right, brother Catholic. I fully agree with you, in a manner. Or rather—well no, I don't. Of course, the baptism makes the child a Christian and saves it, and equally of course without the baptism it is lost, and a person who is lost is only a heathen, and has no right to burial in a Christian cemetery. All that is true, as you say, and as I profess to believe, but it sounds harsh, and our people have a habit of reading and of thinking for themselves. For this reason I do not agree with you, but consider you very heterodox and superstitious in this matter; but it is all right between ourselves."

"Of course," says the Lutheran, "you are both right, and I agree with both of you. We have the true Catholic doctrine in our creed, but our people are a little peculiar, too, and we are obliged, now and then, to pass a resolution in our Synods, denying the evident import of our creed on this subject, just to keep the peace in our Church. But I fully agree with both of you, and also with everybody else. It's a saving ordinance, but there's no real good in it."

"Hold on," cries the Presbyterian, "you are all three utterly wrong, and I can not agree with you at all. Infant baptism has no saving virtue at all, not a bit of it, and you ought to be ashamed to pretend that it has. For my part, I hold that it makes the babe a Christian, and a member of the Church of Christ, and secures to him all the benefits of the covenant of grace. Of course, this amounts to the same thing as your doctrine, but it is not expressed in such a plain, gross way; but the great difference is that my doctrine is true, and yours is not. But, to tell the whole truth, this infant baptism is a childish thing, at best, and I wish we were rid of it."

"Oh, horrors!" cries the Reformed, "that is too bad. Infant baptism is the seal of the covenant, and its value can not be measured, for it makes the babe a partaker of the divine grace, and assures its final salvation. It is a most blessed institution, the hope of the Church, her nursery, as it were. I would not give it up for all the world, but, of course; it is not a saving ordinance. Nobody believes in saving ordinances except the Baptists, who fight infant baptism all the time, declaring there is no authority for it and no virtue in it."

"Well," says the Methodist, "if you are going to give it to the Baptists that's all right, and I will help you; but as for infant baptism, Mr. Wesley expressly says that it washes away original sin, and of course we believe what he says. I confess that it seems to me that whatever washes away original sin must save the soul; but then we do not hold to anything in particular on this subject. We think it is best to baptize infants and run as little risk as possible. You all lay too much stress on it. See here, we are in the main agreed about infant baptism, but do not make its virtues too prominent, or those Baptists will get after us, and make it quite too warm for us. Just be non-committal about it. 'Retain' it in your churches as we do, and let every fellow find out *'vots de good of it?'* for himself."

"For shame!" cries the Congregationalist, "such double-dealing is too bad. There is no virtue in infant baptism, none at all; but it is useful, and would be a great deal more useful than it is, if those Baptists would only let us alone. It secures the benefits of the covenant of grace to the child, and that virtually assures his salvation; but of course he would be just as well off without it. But it enables us to call him a child of the Church, and if we can make him believe it, we can keep him from going off with the Baptists. But of late our people are giving it up at a fearful rate, and we are likely soon to become just like the Baptists in this matter. I tell you infant baptism is a bother, and a constant puzzle, and I almost wish we had never heard of it."

Now, this may seem like a caricature at first glance, but the sober second thought will convince you that it is painfully true to life, and it absolutely does no injustice to our pedobaptist friends, as they will confess, if they read up their own authors faithfully.

Do not turn away and say, "Oh, it is no matter," and then give your influence to support it blindly. Such conduct is unworthy a Christian man. If you love Christ, you love the truth, for he is the *truth*, and all truth is of him and from him, and every several ray of truth leads back to him.

It is our business as Christians to search for truth as for hidden treasures, and, having found it, to honor it and confess it, and show it to others. It is truth, and truth alone, that can make us free from error. If you are a Baptist, let your Baptist light shine out brightly and widely; and if you are not a Baptist, muster up a little courage and look into infant baptism for yourself, and do not rest satisfied until you have answered this crucial question, "*Vot's de good of it?*"

NUMBER III.

"Let Me Alone."

WHILE residing in the village of T——, having occasion to visit a distant city, on my way home I stopped over Sabbath with an old friend. There was a Presbyterian Church in the neighborhood, and I attended worship there. After delivering an able sermon to a large, intelligent and appreciative audience, the pastor invited such parents and friends as desired to have their children baptized to bring them forward. In response to that invitation several persons arose and approached the pulpit, carrying or leading children of various ages, from the babe of three or four weeks to the rather large child of ten or twelve years.

Beginning with the younger ones, the pastor proceeded to administer the ordinance in the usual manner, and without any marked opposition, until he reached the last one, a bright boy of some ten or twelve years. Several little girls had, indeed, exhibited much fear, but under strong parental influence they had finally submitted to the rite, if not reverently, at least tremblingly. Some little boys had exhibited signs of great discontent, but after a few struggles they had accepted the inevitable, with no more tokens of aversion than they might have exhibited if about to be vaccinated. Meantime the last boy in the row watched, with an interest painfully intense, every movement of minister and child.

When his turn came he was almost wild with fear. As the tall, venerable minister approached him he tried to break away; but his father held him so firmly he could not. Finding he must remain, he instantly changed his tactics, springing forward and kicking the minister's shins with great vigor, crying with every kick: "Let me alone! Let me alone!" His father, having a little girl in his right arm, found it very difficult to manage the boy with one hand. Meantime the boy contrived to plant several effective kicks on the ministerial shins, so effective, indeed, that the owner of the shins was glad to retreat out of his reach.

Suddenly the father, with a facial expression not in the highest degree saintly, jerked the boy back several steps. The minister immediately advanced with all boldness, with the sacred water sparkling on the tips of his fingers, but just as he was about to apply it to the boy's head, down went the head and up went the heels belonging to it, colliding with those dear, venerable shins in a most painful way, while the walls in the sacred edifice resounded with the cry: "Let me alone! Let me alone!" Again the prudent minister beat a hasty retreat.

The father, a powerful man, was now thoroughly aroused. With a midnight frown and a mighty wrench he brought that boy upon his feet. Instantly the minister approached, and bending over (he was very tall) he managed to get some two or three drops of water on the devoted head of that belligerent boy, who, in impotent rage, was kicking toward his ghostly benefactor, and screaming his favorite scream: "Let me alone! Let me alone!! Let me alone!!!" As the last scream was solemnly and beautifully punctuated by the official Amen, which ended and confirmed the baptismal formula, and the minister, with a serene, cheerful countenance, re-entered the sacred desk to close the services, I felt—well, my feelings were considerably mixed. To be perfectly frank about it, I had some rather unsanctified feelings just then. In the first place, I always did sympathize with the "under dog," especially when the odds against him were very great. My carnal nature always would rise up and demand fair play. Two men, and one of them a minister, against one poor little boy did seem too much, and I fear I inwardly rejoiced at the boy's wonderful grit.

Another feeling was very strong upon me. I was, for the moment, fairly ashamed of infant baptism. "Is it possible," thought I, "that such an institution is of God? Is it really his will that children shall be forced by human authority to accept the badge of a Christian profession against their earnest protest?" However, I soon comforted myself with the reflection that this was an exceptional case; and I persuaded myself that very few ministers could be found willing to proceed with the baptism under similar circumstances.

But, after all, let me not be unjust. Wherein was it really worse to baptize that boy against his fierce protest than to baptize the helpless, unconscious babe that could not protest, putting upon it a yoke which, in after years, may become a galling, intolerable burden?

All over this land, to-day, are weary hearts hindered from obedience to Christ, in the ordinance of baptism, by the specter of that christening received in infancy; in some cases, perhaps, at my hands. I know an earnest, devoted lady —a true disciple of the Master—to whom her baptism in infancy has been for years a source of deep sorrow. She can not speak of it without tears; yet she does not dare be baptized, lest in so doing she may possibly do wrong. And she is but one of thousands who suffer in the same way and for the same reason. When christened, they were not old enough to protest as that boy did, but they were every whit as grossly outraged as he.

And yet, let us be just; for if infant baptism is indeed of God, my friend did right in baptizing that boy, in spite of his kicks and screams. If God says *do it*, then do it we must, whether children are willing or unwilling. The will of the child and the happiness of the man are never to be set up against a command of God. And when God says *do it*, what right has the parent to say, no, you shall not do it? Can the will of the parent annul the authority of God? Why should a minister desist from a duty which God enjoins, even at the bidding of the parent? Is it right to obey a parent, rather than God? Where has God given the parent power to set aside his solemn ordinances? Or where has he authorized his ministers to waive the adminstration of those ordinances at the behest of any parent? Echo answers, where? where?

Protestant ministers who defend infant baptism

as a divine institution, may well ponder these far-reaching questions. I have a right to say to them, "Gentlemen, why do you disobey God in this matter? If he commands you to do it, why do you not do it? Some of you insist that when Jesus said, 'Go, teach all nations, baptizing them,' he meant baptizing all children, as well as parents. But you do not do that. The homeless bootblack on the street is a child, and as much a member of the nation, as the proud scion of the millionaire, yet you do not baptize him. Why not? In that wretched hovel is a sweet, innocent babe, a daughter of poverty and woe; her father is a drunken outcast, and her mother is an ignorant, irreligious, but almost brokenhearted woman. If your construction of Christ's words be the true one, he has commanded you to baptize *that* babe as truly as the daughter of your well-to-do deacon. Why have you not done it?"

Now, allow me to speak plainly. Either you do not believe your own construction of our Lord's words, or you are guilty of openly contemning his authority. This dilemma has just two horns, as you perceive, and one or the other you must take. Which do you prefer? If the former, you are found guilty of bearing false witness against the Master. If the latter, you are convicted of rank disobedience to his command. It matters little which one you take; either one impales you. As the boy is said to have told the traveler respecting two very bad roads, "No matter, stranger, which one you take; you will soon wish you had taken the other!" Now, gentlemen, look this matter in the face squarely, and harmonize your practice with your creed, if you can. It will not do to throw the blame of a neglect of infant baptism on the parent. That is very commonly done, but without good reason. Ministers of the gospel are certainly commanded to baptize all who are proper subjects of baptism wherever they labor in the gospel. The command is explicit: "Go, teach all nations, baptizing them." This can not mean less than that they shall baptize all who are proper subjects of baptism, in the place where they are teaching or preaching. If, then, infants are to be baptized; if they are proper subjects of baptism; if God actually requires that they be baptized, the ministers are commanded by our Lord himself to baptize them, since they are commanded to baptize all who are proper subjects of baptism, and from this there is no escape.

If the infant, unconscious and involuntary, is, indeed, a proper subject of baptism, then has the minister no choice in the matter; he must baptize him, and the neglect or indifference, or even the opposition, of the parent, can not excuse him. Only such forcible interference as may make the baptism of the child absolutely impossible to the minister, can excuse him for failing to attend to it. Of course, it would be far more pleasant to have the hearty approval of the parent in baptizing the child; but if that approval be wickedly or ignorantly withheld, that does not justify the minister in disobeying God, nor in robbing the dear little babes of whatever blessing, great or small, the baptism might confer. The truth is, the Catholic priests seem to be the most consistent friends of infant baptism. Though they do not pretend that God requires it in his word, even indirectly, yet because the Church requires it, and they regard the Church as his representative and vicegerent on earth, they spare no pains to enforce it, even invoking the aid of the State to compel the people to observe it. And, in this way, every person in a Catholic country reaps whatever benefit there is in it. And if God has really required it, who can blame these men for their zeal? Are they not rather to be honored and commended for it? Why should God be dishonored, and the dear babes be robbed of a great spiritual blessing by allowing a divine ordinance to fall into disuse?

Aye, there's the rub. Is it, after all, a divine institution? Many years ago a venerable minister, fearing I might renounce it altogether, wrote me a very pathetic letter, pleading for it as a divine institution. He insisted that God requires us to baptize infants, but failed to set forth any scriptural proof of such requirement, and then he grew eloquent about its benefits as "a seal of the covenant of grace." Yet, in less than one year afterward, that same minister published an article in the religious press, in which he rejoiced that the members of pedobaptist churches were no longer obliged to have their children baptized, but were at liberty to do as they pleased about it, neglecting it if they chose, without incurring the censure of their church. And still that minister remained an advocate of infant baptism. Can a Christian man really believe an ordinance to be of divine origin and still in full force, and yet rejoice that churches which profess to believe in it, do not censure such of their own members as treat it with neglect?

The fact is, gentle reader, infant baptism has nothing divine about it. God never instituted it, directly or indirectly. In the language of an eminent pedobaptist writer, "Infant baptism was established neither by Christ nor the apostles." Superstition invented it, Romanism adopted and maintained it, and priestcraft continues to cherish it. That is the whole matter in a nutshell. It is neither less nor more than a churchly pre-emption of the child. In it the church puts a mark on the unconscious babe by which to claim it, in after years, as her own. That is all the divinity there is in it. The process is simple and transparent. Baptize the babe when it is wholly in your power, and in after years approach the youth and say: "Ah, my young friend, you belong to us. We baptized you in infancy. You are a child of our church. Come home to your mother."

Here and there the scheme fails—the youth sees through it, or deep convictions of duty oblige him to decide for himself, and let his "mother" mourn her unrequited love; but with tens of thousands it succeeds. This is doubtless the utility which a prominent Congregational minister was thinking of, when, a few years ago, in a sermon on infant baptism, after declaring that there is no warrant of any sort in the Scriptures for it, he said: "I still regard it as a divine institution, just as an ox-yoke is a divine institution. It is useful, just as an ox-yoke is useful; and its utility makes it a divine institution."

Well, it is an ox-yoke affair, only more so; for no humane farmer will yoke up the little calves, and keep the yoke on them through life.

But granting this sort of utility—the utility of an old Romish trick of priestcraft—it is unseemly in the Protestant Church. Look at it soberly. Our Presbyterian brother denounces Romanism, says it is antichrist, the mother of harlots, a scarlet, red handed beast, and many more uncomplimentary but truthful names he applies to her; and his Congregational, Methodist, Lutheran and Episcopal brethren of all sorts, cry amen; and then out they all march in solemn array, and in the name of the Lord proceed to wrap an old rag, filched from the small clothes of that same Romish antichrist, about the brows of the dear babes.

Do not say I am ridiculing sacred things. I am describing a wicked, inconsistent, and most ridiculous thing, and describing it exactly as it is. Mind you, I do not ask pedobaptists to desist from their denunciations of the apostate Romish Church; but in the name of common decency I insist that they should first return the bit of old rag to its rightful owner. It is not fair to denounce Romanism while you wear that dirty Roman rag on your head. Put it away and be consistent. Why should Protestants go about wearing the old rags of Romanism? Why so many persist in doing it is one of the hopeless conundrums of this age.

And yet, there is another feature about this matter even more mysterious.

There are men and women who profess to love Christ and his truth, thousands of them, who will tell you promptly and decidedly that they do not believe in infant baptism at all; that it is not of God; that it is false and foolish; that they would not allow their own children to be baptized under any circumstances; and yet they are members of churches which profess to believe in it, and they habitually give their influence and their money to aid in supporting it. You can find scores and hundreds of such people in every community — Christians, by their own confession, constantly and deliberately contributing to the support of a lie. Does this startle you? Well it may; but it is a plain, undeniable fact, which any one can observe for himself everywhere.

And in multitudes of cases this class of persons contribute so large a proportion of the support of their respective churches that, were they to withdraw it, the church would be obliged to disband. In this way great numbers of pedobaptist churches are now kept up by people who profess a firm confidence that pedobaptism is not of God, while in the same place an evangelical church, which rejects infant baptism, is neglected and starved out.

It is a strange spectacle, indeed. Professed Christians all the time stultifying themselves—forcing upon other children a solemn religious farce which they spurn from their own doors! Have these people a conscience? Well might the children cry out to them, "*Let me alone.*"

NUMBER IV.

"Lint on the Nib."

WHEN I began my work as pastor of the church in the village of T——, I had not given much thought to the communion question. I had, indeed, heard some random talk about it, chiefly denunciations of the supposed bigotry of the Baptists. But, aside from that, I really knew nothing of the subject, and, as a matter of course, I was a zealous open-communionist. I had just one argument, I supposed, and it was extremely short, but, to my untaught judgment, wonderfully conclusive. I stated it to my church in very few words, as follows: "Christ holds fellowship with all Christians, whether baptized or not. He receives men into heaven who were not members of our Church, nor of any other. Why, then, should we refuse to receive such men and commune with them around his table on earth? Is the table holier than heaven? Are we better than our Lord? It is enough that the disciple be *as* his Master. If, therefore, the Master has received a man, and is holding fellowship with him, we, also, ought to receive him at the Lord's table."

This seemed satisfactory to the church, and, with their approval, I habitually invited to the Lord's table all who loved the Master, and everybody said: "How liberal that is! They are a progressive people."

I was a member of an ecclesiastical convention—a sort of hybrid affair, a cross between a Congregational association and a Presbyterian synod, composed of the pastors and delegates of the churches of those two denominations, within certain limits. By way of a little pious fun, we christened the body with two very suggestive titles, either one of which could be used, according to the taste or pleasure of the party using it. A Congregationalist could speak of it as the *"Congreterial Convention;"* and the Presbyterians could denominate it the *"Presbygational Convention."* And this arrangement—originating in sport, and rather mirth-provoking in its nature—had the greater merit of a certain degree of utility, for it gratified the remaining vanity of the dear brethren of both denominations, since it enabled them, each, to put his own denomination before the other without giving any definite offense. Of course, a truly liberal-minded man should not care a fig for his own Church, any more than a generous, neighborly man should care for his own wife and children; but, still, our poor human nature is fearfully set in its ways, and the best of men will sometimes relapse into such utter, awful selfishness as to prefer home to any other place in the wide, wide world. And if the truth were known, it would be found that many of our large-hearted men—leaders in our modern Christian liberality—are not, after all, quite free from the petty weakness of a slight preference for their very own dear Church homes. I am not accusing them of any intentional wrong. In their editorials, and sermons, and speeches, and resolutions, they are no more liberal than they mean to be; but you know that even the stammering and slow of speech find it much easier to preach and resolve than to practice. It should not surprise you, therefore, when eloquent speakers, and writers, and conventionists strike a key a little too high even for their own *advanced* life. Let us not condemn them unduly; rather, let some live Yankee invent some ingenious plan by which a liberal man can still be liberal to his heart's content, and still put his own dear family and Church *just a little ahead* of all others. But pardon this digression, and return with me to our dear old Congreterial Convention.

Our convention met twice each year, and remained in session about three days, occupied with matters devotional, doctrinal, ecclesiastical and literary. We had sermons, essays, speeches discussions, and a good time generally.

It so happened, after I had been at T—— a year or two, that the communion question was somehow brought up in our convention, and open-communion practice was rather pointedly rebuked by some of the brethren. This did not exactly please me, and I looked about with no little interest to see who would arise and vindicate open-communion. But I looked in vain. All who spoke condemned it, and the rest evidently approved all they said, and there seemed to be but one opinion about it in the whole convention.

At last I could endure it no longer, and I arose and told the brethren that I believed in open-communion; that my church believed in it, also; that we constantly practiced it, and that, too, for the very best of reasons; and then I launched my one conclusive argument at them —and sat down.

An aged Presbyterian minister, the venerable and talented Rev. Mr. C., arose and replied. He reminded the convention that he was a warm, true friend of the young brother who had just spoken; and then turning to me, in a most affectionate and fatherly way, he expressed his great surprise and grief at the statements I had so frankly made. Then, characterizing open-communion as utterly unscriptural and thoroughly demoralizing, he paid his respects to my great argument in a way not at all comforting to me. He showed that the very first duty of the believer is to be baptized, and thus make a public confession of his faith in Christ; and that while a man neglects or refuses to do this, we have no right to assume that he is a Christian; that Christ himself sharply rebukes such men for claiming to be his friends, while living in disobedience to his commands, in those awful words: "Why call ye me Lord, Lord, and do not the things that I say?" He next affirmed that the plain duty of every baptized believer is to be a member of the Church, submitting to her discipline, aiding in bearing her burdens, and helping her in pushing on her great work—the evangelization of the world. And then he solemnly affirmed that to invite persons who were neglecting these great duties to sit down to the Lord's table was, practically, to encourage them in their attitude of disobedience to Christ, and to approve their sinful neglect of his Church, and thus to become, in some measure, partakers of their sins.

Somehow he seemed to be talking sound sense and Bible truth all the time, and I inwardly pitied my great argument, he seemed to compress it so much and made it look so small.

After talking half an hour, he turned again to me, begging pardon for saying so much, and stating as his excuse that he had really forgotten himself. But I begged him to go on, as I desired to know and do the truth; and, at my earnest solicitation, he did go on. He proceeded to show that the Lord's table belongs in the Lord's house (the church), and not on the sidewalk in front of it; and that it is a doubtful compliment to the Lord to take his table out of his house for the benefit of those who are unwilling to come into his house. He thought it was lowering the table, and the house, and the Master of the house, at a dreadful rate. (And just between you and me, I thought that he was more than half right. I know I would not thank any one for taking my table out into the street, setting it out there, at my expense, for the benefit of a set of beggars who would not condescend to come into my house; would you? If they claimed to be my friends, I would reply: Then let them show their friendship by coming into my house; wouldn't you?)

He owned that a man ought to be a Christian

before he is baptized or joins the Church, and that he had no doubt in his own mind that there really were Christians outside the Church. (Then I thought he had given himself away; but I soon found he had a way out of it.) He said if we thought a man outside of the Church was a Christian, we could love him and fellowship him as a Christian without inviting him to the Lord's table. He said we did not go to the Lord's table to express our Christian fellowship for each other, but to commemorate his death; and he quoted that Baptist proof-text: "This do in remembrance of me." Somehow he talked in such a way that I would have thought him a narrow, bigoted Baptist, had I not known that he was a straight-laced and very strong Presbyterian. But I very naturally discounted his arguments very largely: First, because he was not a Congregationalist, and, therefore, I could not expect him to be quite as liberal as we were; and, second, because I very much doubted whether he did really believe his own words, for it seemed to me that, if they were really true, they proved too much for a Presbyterian, and demonstrated beyond any reasonable doubt that, after all, the Baptists were right. In this I doubtless did my venerable friend a momentary injustice, since, in fact, there is really no difference of opinion about the Lord's Supper between true Presbyterians and the Baptists; their differences in practice resulting solely from their differences respecting baptism. So true is this that, if a sound, intelligent Presbyterian becomes convinced that the Baptists are right about baptism, he is, forthwith, a thorough-going Baptist without changing his views one iota respecting communion.

My friend, Rev. Mr. C. spoke one hour on the subject; and as that seemed to exhaust his side of it, and as I did not offer any reply, the convention took up other matters.

But in arranging the programme for the next meeting, the brethren appointed me to prepare and read an essay on this question: *"Is it right for a minister of the gospel to invite an unbaptized believer to the Lord's table?"* I put on a brave face to hide my misgivings, and told them to come to the next meeting prepared to surrender, and with a good-natured laugh we adjourned.

I have a philosophic young friend, who is in the habit of observing: "You don't know what is before you," and my experience with that essay illustrates the truth of his remark. I had an idea, when the topic was assigned me, that the brethren were getting me into a pretty tight place, and that I had a particularly hard task before me—an idea which the event very fully confirmed.

But I went about it vigorously, determined to succeed, if it were possible, in setting aside those Presbyterian-Baptistic arguments, for I really dreaded them; knowing very well that if I could not do it, I would be in great danger of becoming a straight-out Baptist, for I had many and very grave doubts about our Presbygational baptism, and they were constantly gaining upon me. So I went to work on my essay under a severe pressure from all quarters. To add to the difficulty of my work, I found my one great argument so badly damaged that I was almost ashamed to use it; and, indeed, an exhaustive search convinced me that I had but little ammunition of any sort available for use. But that only proved the necessity of making the most of what I had, which I proceeded eagerly to do. I took radical ground in respect to the rights of the individual, contending that he alone must be the judge of his duty, as he alone is answerable at the bar of Jehovah for what he does or omits to do. I denied that the Church has a right to require baptism as a condition of membership, or to enforce her opinions respecting the qualifications of communicants at the Lord's table. Of course, in its logical consequences, this would debar the Church from every act of discipline. I winced a little at this, but I could not escape it except by an unconditional surrender, and I was not prepared for that. Yet I could not escape the fact that the Church is responsible for her own conduct as a Church, and I was obliged to meet this question, as one of the inevitable results of the admission of unbaptized persons to the Lord's table and to membership in his Church: "What shall the Church do in the case of any member who may be guilty of a *continuous* neglect of baptism?" I could do no less than to affirm it to be her duty kindly, yet faithfully, to admonish the one guilty of such neglect, and I was obliged to concede also that, her admonition being disregarded, the Church must proceed in due time to withdraw the hand of fellowship from the offender.

Somehow I felt that this was a particularly weak spot in my argument, but I could not help it; the weakness was an inherent one; it belonged inseparably to the position I had felt myself driven to assume, and I resorted to the only remedy left me, heaping up a great pile of mere words, to hide it, if possible, from observation. Finally, I finished my essay and laid it aside, feeling that, all things considered, I had made it a success. But "we do not know what is before us;" at least, I did not, and I am glad of it. I had my little hour of anticipated pleasure, and then came the crash, and my laboriously-planned essay, together with the cause it was intended to promote, went up and out in smoke.

It happened in this way. A few days before the meeting of our convention, I reviewed my essay for the purpose of making verbal corrections and improvements—to put on the finishing touches, as it were. While thus employed, I determined to rewrite the entire paper, introducing in many places forms of expression more elegant, pertinent and forcible. I began this work at once, and had nearly completed it, when I was interrupted by some derangement of my pen. Supposing I had corrected it, I resumed my writing, or attempted to, but my pen would not work properly. Again I stopped, and examining the pen, I found lint on the nib, wedged in, so to speak. While removing the lint, my eye wandered over the unfinished page of manuscript before me, finally resting on the last word I had written—*continuous*—in the question, "What ought the Church to do in the case of any member who may be guilty of a *continuous neglect* of baptism?" *Continuous*, thought I; that is rather an indefinite term. How long is it? Baptism is an evident duty, enjoined by the express command of Christ, sanctioned by his own example, observed by his apostles, and binding on all believers in all ages of the gospel dispensation. It is certainly an imperative duty for every Christian, enforced by the highest authority.

How long, then, may the Church sanction the neglect of it? How long may she innocently acquiesce in a continuous neglect of it? *One year?* No, I dare not affirm that. A whole year of known disobedience! no, that will never do. Well, may she not permit a neglect of it for *six months?* Here I paused and thought a long time. Six months of known disregard of Christ's command, sanctioned by his Church! No, no; that must not be. That is altogether *too continuous.* I dare not approve that. I know it would be wrong. Well, then, say *three months.* But I did not dare to say three months. But surely the Church may wink at a short delay, say *six weeks?* Ah, my dear reader, I was in a very tight place. What could I do? How could I escape? Would God be well pleased with six weeks of known and daring disobedience of his command? Would he be pleased with his Church for winking at so great a sin? If I should counsel the Church to do this thing, would he say to me: "Well done, thou good

BEHIND THE SCENES. 57

and faithful servant; thou hast been faithful over a few things, I will make thee ruler over many things: enter thou into the joy of thy Lord?" I saw clearly that that word *continuous*, which I had used so carelessly, must *go*, and that with it my *whole essay* must also *go*, and that as an honest man I must eat a big batch of humble pie, by publicly renouncing open communion both in theory and practice.

I arose, and taking up my manuscript, I thrust it into the flames. It burned very swiftly and beautifully, and I had the comfort of knowing that it was good for *something*.

In due time I attended the convention, and gladdened the hearts of my Presbyterian and Congregational brethren by confessing myself a convert to close communion. My dear church, after listening to my statement of my reasons for proposing a change in our practice, cheerfully assented, and we were no longer open communion in practice. It was, indeed, a great change, and the passing years confirm in me the conviction that it was a change in the right direction; for, in substance, it was simply a practical recognition of the divine law as supreme.

As I think of the means by which it was brought about, I am astonished. In those youthful days I was very impetuous. I think I had some genuine piety, but I know I was not without a great deal of self-conceit and pride; and, like thousands of better men, I often used words without weighing fully their import. And this is not a slight fault, for words, though impalpable, are things—almost living creatures, I sometimes think—armed with mysterious, wonderful power to wound, or to heal, to enlighten and bless, or to darken and destroy.

No wonder the Master has said: "By thy words thou shalt be justified, and by thy words thou shalt be condemned." He who uses words freely, handles keen-edged tools, and has need of great wisdom and moderation, that he may employ only fitting ones, and arrange them wisely, kindly and well.

And he who writes has need of great circumspection. His pen is an instrument of power. It will trace lines on his own heart not easily effaced. For myself, I often have occasion to recall with gratitude that crisis in my life, when, in the providence of God, all its currents were turned into new channels by "lint on the nib."

NUMBER V.

"*I do not for one moment admit that immersion is valid baptism.*"

AFTER the tragic ending of my essay, I prepared a brief paper, explaining the matter as well as I could, and apologizing for the absence of the expected but defunct defense of open communion. In that paper I affirmed that no person need delay baptism on account of the diversity of views and practices respecting it, since those who could not see the way clearly to accept sprinkling, or pouring, could be immersed, which all Christendom accepts as valid baptism. This simple statement of a fact, which at that time I had never heard controverted, brought my dear old pastor, Rev. Mr. D——, to his feet in an earnest protest. "Sir," said he, "I believe I am a Christian, though a very unworthy one, and I do not for one moment admit that immersion is valid baptism." I was greatly amazed. I looked at him in utter astonishment. I was greatly perplexed, too; for, knowing him intimately, I had never for an instant doubted his piety. Indeed, I had long revered him as a very devoted Christian man, and a faithful and fearless minister. But I also knew facts in his history that seemed irreconcilable with this strange, sweeping statement. I gazed at him in silence some moments, hardly knowing what reply to make. There was a large congregation present. It was in his own church, and I was standing in his pulpit, while he stood near the center of the room. Every eye seemed fixed on him, and the silent suspense soon became painful. At last I said: "Bro. D——, may I ask you one question?" "Certainly," said he. "Bro. D——," said I, "if immersion is not valid baptism, why did you lead your own daughter, who had been sprinkled in infancy, into the river and immerse her, saying: 'I baptize thee in the name of the Father, and of the Son, and of the Holy Ghost?" If immersion is not valid baptism, how could you do that?" It was now his turn to remain silent, which he did for some time, meanwhile apparently engaged in an earnest study of the toes of his boots. At last he looked up and said: "I did it to please my daughter. I did not regard it as baptism, but she did; and I did it to please her."

Just then a Presbyterian minister arose and

said: "Sir, look at me. I do not admit that immersion is valid baptism." I did look at him, but having no personal kowledge of his practice in respect to baptism, I contented myself with this remark: "My dear Bro. L——, I am sorry for you." Yet I have since known persons whom Bro. L—— had immersed. It is true, he did not like to do it; but when they said: "We must be immersed, and if you will not immerse us, we will go to the Baptists," he replied, "Oh, well, rather than have you go to the Baptists, I will immerse you." And he did.

I do not know of one evangelical church of any denomination which will not receive a Baptist as a baptized person. I do not say there is no church that would refuse to receive him as baptized, for this is a wide world, and there may be a church, or a sort of one, somewhere in some out-of-the-way nook or cranny, that would actually refuse to receive an honest, upright Baptist on his immersion, and would require him to be sprinkled. If anybody on earth knows of such a church, I would be glad to have him publish the fact, together with the name and location of the church, and its reasons for a course so very singular.

It is said our Presbyterian brethren have been known to depose a minister for immersing a person, and it may actually be true that they have done so; but I never yet knew a Presbyterian Church to refuse membership to a Baptist because he had been immersed, nor to require him to be sprinkled as a condition of admission among them. The truth is, that immersion, as baptism, is like gold coin—current everywhere, in all the churches.

Almost as a matter of course, those who persist in the practice of sprinkling do all they dare do to discredit immersion, casting contempt upon it, and, in many cases, refusing to administer it; but I know of none who have the hardihood to say that those who have been immersed upon a profession of faith are not baptized. Even my old pastor, who so stoutly declared, "I do not for one moment admit that immersion is valid baptism," was in the habit of receiving immersed persons into his church as properly baptized.

I have often been astonished at the hostility manifested toward immersion by men who, at the very same time, are in the habit of recognizing it as valid baptism whenever it knocks for admission into their respective folds. And yet the motive is usually evident. A young lady, whose family are Congregationalists, became a regular attendant at our church (Baptist), and everything moved along very pleasantly—her family being among my warm personal friends—until she became an earnest Christian, and applied for baptism and membership with us. Then there was a commotion in the camp. Her family positively forbade her uniting with the Baptist Church. They would consent to her being immersed, but not by a Baptist minister, nor to join a Baptist Church. After many days of unavailing pleading and tears, finding she could not change their resolution, she reluctantly went to the Methodist Church (there was no Congregational Church in the town), and was immersed by the pastor. I was present at her baptism, as were many hundreds more, and the manner in which it was conducted was an outrage almost insufferable.

Arriving at the river bank, near the center of the town, the minister instantly marched into the water with a determined sort of stride, as if he were impatient to the last degree and determined to get through with a disagreeable job as speedily as posssible. He kept his hat on his head, and, without waiting for a word of prayer, or any religious services whatever, he led the poor girl into the water, and, halting where it was not more than two-thirds the proper depth, he hurriedly uttered the baptismal formula and then fairly hurled her under the water, as if in anger; then, jerking her out, he led her to the shore, and, without removing his hat, dismissed the people with the briefest sort of a benediction.

And yet the weather was pleasant, and there was plenty of time for the proper and decorous observance of the ordinance. He evidently did not intend to observe it in a decorous manner, lest others might be impressed by it, and come to regard it as the scriptural baptism. In other words, he meant to heap contempt upon immersion, which yet he received as baptism.

He intended to neutralize the influence of immersion as much as possible by his method of administration, and his desire to defend sprinkling prompted that intention.

And for the same reason the family of the girl consented that she should receive immersion at his hands rather than mine. They had been, and continued to be, my warm friends; but they knew that immersion by a Baptist minister, in connection with a Baptist Church, means something—means a condemnation and rejection of sprinkling—and they had been sprinkled. Their refusal of her request for permission to receive baptism at my hands, and to unite with our church, was neither less nor more than an impotent effort to justify themselves in having received sprinkling as baptism.

But they also knew that immersion by a Methodist minister, in connection with the Methodist Church, means only a concession to the opinions and choice of the candidate; and they probably knew, also, that that Methodist minister, like too many others, would take care to make it mean just as little as possible, even by way of such concession. Such motives, I grant you, are not remarkable for their Christian tone; but such as they are, they are far more common, and far more potent, than many good people imagine.

A few years ago, Rev. Mr. B——, a Methodist Presiding Elder, was called to officiate in a Methodist Church, in one of the beautiful interior cities of Ohio, on a certain occasion when a large number of persons were to be baptized. What he did, and how he did it, I will tell you, as he told it to me, and in substantially the same words:

"It was our quarterly meeting, and being Presiding Elder of that district, it was my duty to preach, and knowing that there were a large number of persons to be baptized that day, I resolved to speak on baptism. You know that by the rules of our Church we are required to give each candidate his choice of modes; and we immerse, sprinkle or pour each one, as he may elect. I had some fear lest a few might that day choose to be immersed, and I did not want to immerse them, if I could, in any reasonable way, avoid it. So I proceeded to show, as well as I could, that sprinkling is the proper mode, but I could not make it so clear as I desired; so I turned to immersion, and said all I could think of to discredit the practice. I called attention to the great inconvenience of it at all times, and especially to ladies, and to the absolute discomfort and danger of it in cold weather. I enlarged upon this, describing the cutting of the ice, the crowds shivering in the chilling wintry winds, the poor Baptist preacher standing in the ice-water, chilled to the very bones, his arms encrusted with ice, and his teeth chattering with cold, and the forlorn candidates struggling and choking amid the floating ice, or trembling in their frozen garments until the close of the service. I then spoke of the manifest impropriety of the immersion of ladies by gentlemen, and in a promiscuous crowd, and related a number of anecdotes to illustrate the great indecencies, always liable to occur on such occasions.

"My sermon was received with a very marked interest throughout, and I fancied no one would care, in the very face of it, to ask for immersion. But alas! I soon found that this was only a fancy; for a very large majority of the candidates—among the number many excellent ladies—insisted on being immersed, and I was obliged to march at the head of that congregation to the river and there immerse them. Well, I got through it somehow; but from that day to this I have never preached on baptism, and I think my call to preach upon it has run out."

This confession speaks for itself, and tells the whole tale; and for my part, I honor Mr. B—— for his frankness in the matter. Yet he told it to me as a capital joke on himself. He did not seem to see anything morally wrong in the part he had taken in the matter. And yet he is a good man in my judgment, and in the estimation of all who know him well. In respect to baptism, he is simply blinded and warped by the pernicious, unscriptural usage and views of his Church. Doubtless, he entered that Church in early life, or at least before he had examined the question of baptism with anything like thoroughness; and having accepted things as he found them, he was slowly, but surely, molded into conformity with them. And as time passed on he became fixed and firmly set in his niche and notions, and when occasion required, he made the best defense of his practice that the case admits of; for, ridiculous as it is, no man can improve on it.

In the language of an old friend, a Congregational minister, addressed to me, "Don't you know, sir, that every person we pedobaptists immerse is just so much capital for the Baptists?" This friendly reprimand was provoked by my action in the case of two ladies, recent converts under my ministry, who desired me to give them the reasons why they should be sprinkled. I refused to do so, bidding them study the Bible for themselves, and telling them frankly that it was enough for me to sprinkle them, if they should require it at my hands. "But," said I, "examine the matter for yourselves, and when your minds are made up let me know, and I will sprinkle you, or I will immerse you, whichever you may prefer."

The ladies finally decided that, as I was willing to sprinkle them if they desired it, I must regard sprinkling as scriptural and right; and that, being a minister, and engaged constantly in the study of such matters, I must know all about it; and that the weather being exceedingly cold, it would be much more comfortable to be sprinkled; and so they requested me to sprinkle them, which I did. But I had urged them to decide for themselves, by the study of the Bible, and my friend very justly regarded that as a risky business for the friends of sprinkling, as indeed it is. I knew that, when I did it, and I secretly hoped the ladies would choose to be sprinkled, for I dreaded to go into the water to immerse, fearing that I could not do it; but I was actually afraid to advise them to be sprinkled lest, after all, it might be wrong.

Immersion not valid baptism! That is strange, indeed; strange that any good man ever could affirm it; stranger still if one single Christian man could anywhere be found who actually believed it. The truth is that immersion lies upon the very surface of the Scripture text, while sprinkling, if it be there at all, is buried so deep that even the most learned men can not find it. A young lady, just converted to Christ, came to her mother in great distress, saying, "Mother, is sprinkling in the Bible?" "Certainly, my daughter." Her mother was a Presbyterian. "Mother, please find it for me." The mother searched for it, but in vain. She said: "Daughter, I know it is there, but I can not find it. I will ask our minister to find it when he comes." In a few days he came, and the mother preferred her request: "Is sprinkling in the Bible?" "Why, of course it is," said he. "Well, my daughter asked me to find it for her, and I thought I could, but after looking a long time I could not. Will you please to find it for us?" "Yes; hand me the Bible." She handed it to him, and as he turned over the leaves he engaged the mother in an earnest conversation about other matters, until baptism was quite forgotten, and then he rose and left the house. The next time he came his attention was again called to the subject, and once more he took the Bible to look up sprinkling. But this time the mother, fully aroused, was not to be eluded so easily. She pressed him closely, and at last he rose and left, saying, "Yes, sprinkling is in the Bible, but it takes a great deal of learning and time to find it."

A gentleman, whose attention was arrested by the fact that converted Indians are very apt to become Baptists, inquired of one of them why it was so. The Indian, after thinking a moment, replied: "Well, I don't know, unless it is that we poor Indians, being generally ignorant people, are obliged to take the Book just as it reads." Ah, that is the secret of it, and that, too, is one of the best proofs that Baptists are right. For the dear old Bible is the book of the people, written in the language of every-day life. Jesus, sending John the tokens of his own Messiahship, bid the men to tell him, "The *poor* have the gospel preached unto *them*." And to-day one of the best tokens of the divinity of the Bible is the fact that the masses of the people, the common people, can read it and understand it for themselves without the intervention of scribe or pharisee, priest or Pope. I do not decry learning (God forbid), but I call attention to the fact that the Bible speaks to the unlearned as distinctly and clearly as to the most highly cultured. It is the people's book, and so long as it is in their hands and they are at liberty to read it for themselves, the truth has nothing to fear, and ultimate triumph is certain.

The time was when immersion, as baptism, was on trial, and those who accepted it did so at their peril; but that day has passed away never to return, and to-day sprinkling and pouring are on trial, and the trial is going against them at a tremendous rate. Already it is a difficult matter to find competent men who are willing to attempt their defense, while scores of their best friends frankly admit that they have no case at all. Here and there, perhaps, one may still be found willing to rise up and say that immersion is not valid baptism; but even they actually receive it and treat it as valid in the most solemn business of the Church. But, on the other hand, millions tell you in the most emphatic manner possible that immersion is not only baptism, but the only valid water baptism, while other millions insist on immersion as the only baptism satisfactory to them. Two hundred years ago men were ostracizing Baptists for the practice of immersion; to-day the descendants of those same men are hastening to put baptisteries into their churches.

NUMBER VI.

"I will go to the bottom of this matter, and find out the truth if I can; and wherever that leads me I will cheerfully go."

AFTER a residence of several years in the village of T—— my health failed, and I was obliged to leave my dear people and enter a field where my labors would not be so severe. Accordingly I removed to the village of M——, with the understanding that I should preach but once a week, and that I should spend the most of my time in the saddle—in search of health.

When I had been there some five or six months, business called me to a distant city for a few days. While there a friend, a Congregational divinity student, gave me a little anonymous book, filled with extracts from various pedobaptist works on the subject of baptism.

As he handed it to me he laughingly observed that he had not read it himself, but that the Baptist brother who gave it to him would gladly give him another, and that it might serve to amuse me and while away an idle hour. I put it in my pocket, and did not think of it again until some days after my return home.

Sitting in my study one day, somewhat wearied with the labor of preparation for the next Sabbath, and wishing for something diverting to read, I suddenly recollected the little book my friend had given me. I got it and sat down to read. Oh, horrors! Here was diversion with a vengeance. The book was literally packed with extracts from pedobaptist writers, containing the most damaging admissions of the correctness of the Baptist views. My mind, already sorely pressed with doubts about infant baptism and sprinkling, was instantly greatly agitated.

If we were right, why did our champions make such fatal admissions? Surely a man defending his own practice would admit nothing against it which he did not deem to be true. But here were some of our greatest writers giving our cause away completely. Did they know that we really have no valid defense? Did they, after all, know that the Baptists are right? It certainly seemed so.

But hold! This is a book gotten up by some Baptist, thought I, and he has garbled these extracts, doctoring them up to suit his own purposes. Doubtless he misrepresents these writers, or, rather, makes them misrepresent themselves by a skillful but dishonest arrangement of their sentences. This notion gave me a little relief. But just then my eye rested on an extract from the "*Systematic Theology of Storr and Flatt,*" which began by stating that the original baptism was probably immersion, since the apostles could understand our Lord's command in no other way than as enjoining an immersion of the body in water.

That Storr and Flatt—great Lutheran theologians—could ever have published such stuff, was to me utterly incredible. I dashed the book upon the floor, crying out in great indignation: "I wish those Baptists could tell the truth." Instantly I recollected that I had, but a few days before, added the work of Storr and Flatt to my library. I ran across the room and clutched the volume whence the extract purported to have been taken, and returned to my chair, saying, as I did so: "I will expose that lie." Opening the volume at the page indicated in the little book, I sat many minutes fairly dumb with astonishment. This is what I read in the great work of Storr and Flatt. You will find it in their *Biblical Theology,* vol. II., art. Baptism page 290, edition 1826:

"*The primitive mode was probably by immersion.* The disciples of our Lord could understand his command in no other manner than as enjoining immersion: for the baptism of John, to which Jesus himself submitted, and also the earlier baptism of the disciples of Jesus, were performed by dipping the subject into cold water.

"And that they actually did understand it so is proved, partly by those passages of the New Testament which evidently allude to immersion, ... and partly from the fact that immersion was so customary in the ancient Church, that even in the third century the baptism of the sick, who were merely sprinkled with water, was entirely neglected by some, and by others was thought inferior to the baptism of those who were in health, and who received baptism, not merely by aspersion, but who actually bathed themselves in water. This is evident from Cyprian (*Epist.* 69, *ed. Bremar*, p. 185, etc.) and Eusebius (*His. Eccles. L.*, vi., cap. 43), where we find the following extract from the letter of the Roman bishop, Cornelius: 'Novatus received baptism on a sick bed by aspersion (perichutheis), f it can be said that such a person received baptism.' No person, who had during sickness been baptized by aspersion, was admitted into the clerical office. Moreover, the old custom of immersion was also retained a long time in the Western Church—at least in the case of those who were not indisposed.

"Under these circumstances, it is certainly to be lamented that Luther was not able to accomplish his wish with regard to the introduction of immersion, as he had done in the restoration of wine in the eucharist. But it is evident that there was a very important difference between the two cases.

"After the restoration of the wine, the laity could partake of both bread and wine in the celebration of the supper of our Lord. But, on the contrary, if immersion had at that time been restored, whatever course those who had been baptized by aspersion might pursue, whether they were contented with their baptism by aspersion, or incurred the danger of disobeying Christ's precept by being baptized twice, they would have been harassed by doubts and fears, which it would have been difficult, and, perhaps, in most cases, impossible to remove. Happily, however, the change of the ancient custom of immersion, although it ought not to have been made, destroys nothing that is essential to this ceremony, as it was instituted by our Savior."

Now study this long extract and note its amazing admissions, and then realize, if you can, my situation. Here were at least five of our greatest pedobaptist scholars and theologians affirming all that the much-abused Baptists claim as to what baptism is. Note their affirmations:

I. That Christ commanded immersion.

II. That his command could not be understood by the apostles in any other way.

III. That Christ himself was immersed in water.

IV. That his apostles really did understand his command to enjoin immersion, and that they obeyed it by immersing.

V. That immersion was the practice of the whole Church in primitive times.

VI. That immersion continued the general practice in the Western (or Romish) Church a long time.

VII. That it was finally supplanted by sprinkling—a change which ought not to have been made.

VIII. That Luther desired to restore immersion in baptism, but could not.

IX. That his failure to restore it is to be regretted.

And now remember that these are the admissions, or rather the affirmations, of five great pedobaptist theologians, made in a standard work on theology. They are the statements of Drs. Storr and Flatt, published without a word of dissent by Dr. Schmucker, aided by Moses Stuart and Prof. Murdock. These are all men of the greatest eminence, renowned for learning and ability. They belong, it is true, to the last generation, but they have few peers among the men of to-day. And they affirm substantially that the Baptists are right, and sprinkling is, indeed, an innovation, and an unfortunate one. Do you wonder that I was overwhelmed, and most thoroughly confounded? At first I thought an unconditional surrender was the only thing left me, as an honest man. But presently I considered that these great men might, after all, be mistaken; that possibly they had sold themselves for nought, and I resolved that they should not sell me. I would examine the matter for myself. But why should I? Why not dismiss the whole matter and keep right along in my present practice! If I was wrong, I was in respectable and pious company. If it was a sin, hosts of good men were guilty of it, and surely I could stand it if they could! Why think about it! But I could not help thinking about it.

Here were great men, whom the world revered as good men, deliberately publishing a virtual confession that, in the matter of a solemn Christian ordinance, they and their churches were habitually disobeying the command of our Lord.

Would their daring disobedience excuse me in pursuing the same course? Could I plead their example? And if at the last it should appear, to their shame and confusion, that Christ does make a difference between those who obey him and those who do not. would it gratify me to be a partaker of their condemnation? If they were, as indeed they seemed to be, blind leaders, would their reputation prevent their falling into the ditch? Could I afford to be a blind follower of such blind leaders? But was I not also, in a more humble way, a leader? Were not many following me with implicit confidence in my wisdom and integrity? What right had I to abuse their confidence by a willing or willful ignorance? Then the authority of my Lord, was that to be set at nought, or to be lightly esteemed by his professed disciples? But then came the thought, urged by so many as an excuse for a neglect to look into this matter, or, having looked into it, for continuing to support the practice of sprinkling contrary to the divine command: "Oh, it is only an outward form, anyway!" Only an outward form—that is true, *but it is an outward form that Christ himself commands us to observe*—if these great pedobaptist witnesses are correct. If he really commands me to observe this outward form, then neglect of it is disobedience to his command. In rejecting the form he has enjoined, I reject his authority. Am I ready to do that? If I do it, how can I call him Lord? Will he not reply, "Why call ye me Lord, Lord, and do not the things which I say?"

Finally the struggle in my mind took form: Suppose I can find out the truth about this matter, what will I do about it? What ought I to do about it? Suppose I learn that Jesus did actually enjoin immersion, am I bound to obey his injunction? Am I willing, in that case, to reject sprinkling?

Over this issue I wrestled three days in agonizing prayer. Then came a clear, settled, firm conviction that it was my duty, at any cost, thoroughly to investigate the whole question of baptism, and to yield obedience to the expressed will of Jesus, whenever I had clearly learned what that will is, or cease to call him Lord. And with that conviction of duty came also a sense of consecrated strength, and a confidence of divine help in doing it.

Then I firmly resolved that, "God being my helper, I will go to the bottom of this matter, and find out the truth, if I can, and wherever that leads I will cheerfully go."

You wonder, perhaps, that it should have cost

me a struggle so severe, and so prolonged, to arrive at a resolution so evidently just and so clearly demanded by every principle of loyalty to Christ in every case of honest doubt respecting duty. I have often wondered at it myself, for I regarded Christ as King all that time. But my situation was peculiar. I had long been accustomed to hear baptism spoken of as a "mere form;" its outward conditions as altogether indifferent; its form a matter of personal choice; and that, whatever Christ might have enjoined, he was evidently well pleased with those who were sprinkled, since he constantly blessed them and their labors in his vineyard. I had also great personal interests at stake. I was a minister in a denomination greatly endeared to me. The thought of a possible separation from it was intensely painful. I was pastor of a small but lovely church. Our numbers had already doubled since my settlement with it. Not one discordant note marred our perfect harmony. Our prospects were very bright. I was bound up in my church by ties exceedingly strong. Among our own people I had a wide acquaintance, and hosts of warm friends outside my own parish. I was a young man, and not without that laudable ambition to enlarge my sphere of usefulness which ought to animate the breast of every young man. But that was not all, nor the greatest of my difficulties. The outcome of a thorough examination might be Baptistic, and I shrank from the thought of becoming a Baptist. And I dreaded, too, the idea of a change, lest I might be called a turn-coat, and be regarded as a fickle sort of man, unstable in my ways; a reputation well-nigh fatal to ministerial success, no matter how little it may be merited.

These are the great influences that held me back; but, thank God, through his grace, they were at last overcome, and I entered resolutely upon the dreaded investigation and carried out fully my solemn resolution, though it cost me all the changes and sacrifices I so much feared. For many weary months I studied, and thought, and prayed; examining rigidly every argument for and against sprinkling and infant baptism. I read scores of our own authors, and traveled many scores of miles to confer with our ablest champions. I resolutely refused to read a Baptist book, or to confer with any member of any Baptist church, or with any of their ministers. In this way I sought to avoid the danger of being influenced by personal feelings, or personal appeals. It was a rather one-sided plan, I must confess, but it seemed the best thing for me to do; and I do not regret it. Day by day the mists cleared away. Day by day the truth became more evident, and more firmly established. At length I could no longer doubt. I was fully, thoroughly convinced that we were wrong and the Baptists were right. Reluctantly I severed my connection with my dear people and went out from among them, bearing with me their benedictions, and most precious memories of their brotherly kindness.

And though the way was painful, I am glad God led me thus. I am not harassed by doubts whether I am doing right when I immerse one who professes faith in the Lord Jesus. I can confidently invoke the presence of the Master at a baptismal scene, for I know by a blessed experience that he delights to honor his own ordinance, and to put a difference between that which he has commanded and the invention of men, which, with so many, has usurped its place. Many years have passed away, bringing me enlarged facilities for a more thorough study of this subject, and, year by year, the evidence continues to accumulate, until I am amazed that I could have had any doubt about it.

And yet men go on making sport of immersion, and putting sprinkling in its place, just as blindly as I once did. I pray that God may lead them to test the practice by his holy word;

for when a man resolves, "By the grace of God, I will go to the bottom of this matter, and find out the truth, if I can, and wherever that leads I will cheerfully go," he is sure to become a Baptist.

I am not a prophet, nor do I belong to the honored family of the prophets, but I venture the prediction that one hundred years hence no one will pretend that sprinkling is baptism; that the practice of it will be unknown among evangelical Christians; that it will be a part of the almost-forgotten rubbish of a less enlightened past, which antiquarians will occasionally explore, much as they now search the Catacombs of ancient Rome, or the rock tombs of ancient Egypt. And the preachers of that period will occasionally allude to it, only to point a moral, to demonstrate man's need of divine guidance under all circumstances.

Now, do not turn up your classic nose and say, "Oh, pshaw!" Just wait and see; and if it isn't so, just come and tell me; and I will not only concede the failure of my prophecy, but I will also lament the wickedness of good men in persisting so long in their disobedience to the command of Christ, and their folly in preferring an invention of men to an ordinance of God; and I will insist then, as now, that immersion is the only valid baptism.

NUMBER VII.

"If you are determined to go to the bottom of this matter, you will come out a Baptist; there is no help for that."

I HAD been engaged in the study of baptism about four weeks, and daily our practice seemed more and more unscriptural and indefensible. I was in a sad plight. I did not dare to give up the investigation, for a solemn vow obliged me to continue it. And, besides, I desired most earnestly to know and do the truth, and the truth only. But to find the truth in this case, I must search for it. It seemed to be buried beneath a vast heap of rubbish, which must be removed. But, on the other hand, each day increased the probability, in my mind, that I would ultimately be obliged to give up both sprinkling and infant baptism, and with them my church and denomination, and go over to the Baptists; and it seemed impossible to do that. I was very much in the condition of that mystical man who is said to have caught a bear by the fore paws. If the legend be true, the bear was in the act of descending a tree. His hind feet had just touched the ground, while his fore feet were on either side of the tree. At that critical moment the endangered rustic caught those paws and held them fast, the while crying lustily for help. But, alas! no one heard his cries, and no help came. Time moved on, doubtless with leaden feet, in the opinion of the rustic; but without bringing relief to the poor man. He did not dare let go, and it seemed impossible to hold on a moment longer. If the legend may be trusted, the man was in a worse condition than the bear. How that man got out of the scrape, would be a very interesting bit of history, if only it were well written—that is, if he ever got out of it at all. Here I was, grappling a problem which threatened my overthrow, yet I could not let go my hold. I am sure I earnestly desired help—effective help—and, at last, I thought it had surely come.

I learned one day that Rev. Dr. S——, an able Presbyterian minister, had just arrived in our town on a vacation trip, and that he intended to remain several days. I immediately sent him an invitation to occupy my pulpit the next Sabbath, and he accepted it, and then left town on a short hunting trip, from which he returned on Saturday evening. I did not succeed, therefore, in getting a personal interview with him until just before the hour of service on Sabbath morning. I met him at the church, and requesting him to step aside for a few moments' conversation, I told him about my trouble, saying that I had made a solemn vow to go to the bottom of the matter; that I had been studying it earnestly and prayerfully, almost day and night, for four weeks, and that the ground seemed to be slipping away from under me, and that, unless I could get help, I would be obliged to give up sprinkling and infant baptism, and ended by asking him earnestly to help me. He listened calmly until I stopped; and knowing, as I did, that he was a man of culture and of much ability, I confidently expected immediate aid.

What sort of aid he gave me will appear from his reply, which I give verbatim:

"I am sorry to hear you talk so, for if you are determined to go to the bottom of this matter, you will come out a Baptist; there is no help for that, and I regret it, for I hate close communion so. If you have studied this subject four weeks, you know more about it than I do, for I never studied it at all, and I never will. I was born a Presbyterian, I was brought up a Presbyterian, I have lived a Presbyterian, and I mean to die a Presbyterian. Of course, we had these subjects in the theological seminary, but I gave no thought to them. I have never allowed myself to entertain any doubt about the correctness of our practice, and I never will. I think I love infant baptism so well that I could not give it up, even if I knew it to be wrong. As for myself, I am resolved never to admit any question about it; but for you, with your resolution to go to the bottom of it, there is but one result possible—you must come out a Baptist. I know enough about the matter to know that; and I am sorry it is so, for I hate close communion."

This strange, astounding speech seemed to take away my breath, and my power of utterance, for a few moments. I was amazed, grieved, nay, almost stupefied by it. At last, regaining in some degree my self-control, I said to him:

"My dear sir, how dare you talk in this manner? You are a public teacher—a minister of the gospel—and your people look to you for instruction in divine things; and here is a question dividing the people of God in a dreadful manner, causing discord in families, and separating many who otherwise would be firm friends, bringing great scandal on the cause of Christ, and very bitter grief to many Christian hearts—and yet you declare that you have never sought to know the truth about it, and that you never will. But all this time you have taken sides in this controversy, maintaining firmly before the public that your side is right and the other side wrong, when, in fact, for aught you know, your side is altogether wrong! And your people are saying: 'We can not be wrong, for Bro. S. is an educated man, and a good man, and he is confident we are right.'

"And with this great responsibility on you, you deliberately refuse to look into the matter. You resolutely shut your eyes that you may not see, and stop your ears that you may not hear. By your own statement, you willfully shut out the light, and make yourself, on this subject, a blind leader. I ask you, sir, how you dare to do this thing? How can you take this fearful responsibility?"

He replied, quite unmoved:

"Well, sir, I have taken this responsibility so far, and I intend to continue taking it to the end; and if you do not choose to take the same responsibility, you will have to be a Baptist; that is all there is of it."

Just then the church bell rang, and our interview ended. We went into the pulpit together, and in due time he unrolled his manuscript and read a very beautiful sermon on "The Conditions of Growth in Grace." In eloquent periods he insisted that every Christian should keep his mind open to the truth; no matter whence it might come, no matter how unpopular it might be, no matter how unpalatable it might be to him. He dwelt, in glowing sentences, on the necessity of candor and impartiality in the investigation of truth; and heartiness in its reception when once its claim to be received had been fairly vindicated.

My people drank in the sermon much as a thirsty ox drinks in the cold water; thinking, doubtless, "What an earnest, heroic truth-lover is this! Would that we were more like him!"

And I listened, fairly dazed and overwhelmed. "How can he point out the way so clearly," thought I, "and at the same time refuse to walk in it himself! Does he not know that every sentence he utters condemns his own practice? Is he not an arrant, determined hypocrite? Oh, God! is there truth among men? Can I ever again have any confidence in men?"

It was, to me, a severe ordeal, indeed; and I was exceedingly glad when the service ended, and I was at liberty to return home. But I carried with me a burdened heart, and resumed my studies in deep sorrow.

And, yet, as the days moved on, I found in

my soul a growing purpose to meet the issue manfully. I would "buy the truth, and sell it not." No matter what it cost, I would have it, if attainable. Did not Jesus say, "If ye abide in my word, then are ye truly my disciples; and ye shall know the truth, and the truth shall make you free?" Did he not pray, "Sanctify them in the truth; thy word is truth?" Did he not come into the world to "bear witness to the truth?" Does he not declare of himself, "I am . . . . the truth?"

Why, then, should I shrink from the truth, and put my friendships among men above the truth of God? To do so were to confess myself disloyal to Christ, and unworthy of him. No; I will not do it. Whatever may come, I will be true to Christ; true to the great trust reposed in me as a public teacher of gospel truth; true to truth, which alone is imperishable; true to my own conscience and to my own manhood. Thus the very utterances intended to frighten me away from the dangerous investigation served only to show me more distinctly the importance of it, and the urgent need of a fearless manliness and impartiality in conducting it. As an immediate result, I drew nearer to Christ, resting on him more completely than ever for the needed wisdom and strength; and, assured of his favor and guidance, entered into the examination before me with greater zeal and resolution than ever.

Presently one of my brethren came to me and said:

"I had a conversation with Rev. Dr. S—— on our way home from church Sabbath morning, respecting your case."

"Indeed," said I; "tell me about it."

"Well," he replied, "I inquired whether, in his opinion, there is any good reason why you should be so troubled about baptism.

"He said: 'No, none whatever; the matter is all plain enough.'

"Then I said: 'Bro. S——, can sprinkling and infant baptism be clearly proven from the Bible?'

"'Certainly,' said he, 'there is no doubt about it at all.'

"That encouraged me greatly, and I said: 'Bro. S——, I am glad it is so; and I want you to give me the proof-texts, so that I can show them to our pastor; for we love him and do not want to lose him.'

"'Well,' said he, 'the fact is, I am a little rusty on this subject just now, for I have not given it much attention for a long time, and therefore I can not comply with your request;

but when I get home I will send you a book which sets the matter in a clear light, and you can hand that to your pastor and request him to read it, and it will set him right.'

"I charged him not to forget it, and he assured me he would not. I expect the book in a few days, and when it comes, I will send it to you immediately, and I want you to read it very carefully; for, my dear brother, we want you to remain with us. We can not spare you."

I promised to read the book with great care, as soon as possible, and he went away very hopeful about the result. In a day or two after this interview the book came, and I sat down at once to a diligent study of it. I had already examined a large number of books written in defense of sprinkling and infant baptism, but this one I had never seen. I gave it three earnest, searching examinations, going over each sentence, each time, with the greatest care, hoping I might somewhere discover some ground of hope of a final vindication – or, at least, of a reasonable excuse for our practice in baptism. Alas! I was keenly disappointed; the book was weaker than any I had before read. It abounded in misinformation, false statements and transparent sophistry.

Taking my pencil, I wrote in a fly-leaf: "I

have read many defenses of our baptismal practices, all of them defective and inconclusive at best, but this exceeds all others in weakness and wickedness, abounding, as it does, in statements which the author must have known were false when he wrote them; and in pretended arguments which he must have known were transparent sophistries, at the very moment he penned them;" and then returned the book to my friend.

Now I am not an accuser of the brethren, but I venture this remark: That the mass of our pedobaptist brethren are not very unlike my friend, Rev. Dr. S——. They would probably shrink from a plain avowal of the fact—but still it is a fact—that they do not examine this matter candidly, impartially and exhaustively. Among the multitudes of pedobaptist brethren whom I have the honor to know, more or less intimately, I can not recall five who have ever given this subject an honest, thorough examination. If a pedobaptist brother is indignant at this statement, and disposed to challenge its accuracy, let him stand up, and in the presence of God solemnly affirm that he has himself given it a full, candid and thorough investigation. And if he can do that, then let him name four others —pedobaptist ministers—who dare make the same solemn affirmation for themselves; and after he has done that, then let him assail my statement, if he deems it wise to do so. The truth is, the strongest defense of sprinkling and infant baptism that can be written by mortal man will not bear an honest, critical examination, and the long history of attempted defenses is only a sad recital of so many able failures.

Learning in the dear school of an experience so painful, the leaders of the pedobaptist forces have adopted new and peculiar tactics—tactics admirable, perhaps, among the various devotees of the pagan idols, but sadly out of place and out of character among a Christian people—the tactics of indifference.

"Oh, it is no matter. One way is as good as another." "No, I never took the trouble to investigate baptism. It is not worth while. It is only a form, anyway." "No, thank you, I will not try to study this question. Sprinkling will do just as well as immersion, and I like it a great deal better; and I am satisfied." "No, I don't care about baptism. It's only a form, and I prefer the realities of religion." "Oh, baptism is nothing. I do not think about it. I believe in holiness and communion with Jesus. That's enough for me." "Well, we are all going to the same heaven, and it don't matter what road we take, so we get there."

These, and a thousand more of similar tenor, are the expressions which greet you from the lips of the laity of pedobaptist churches when you press the command of Christ upon them, and insist that they ought to obey it in the only way possible, by being duly immersed. And they all mean just one thing—indifference to his command. And their pastors, as a rule, encourage this spirit of indifference, telling them it really makes no sort of difference whether they are sprinkled or immersed; yet, at the same time, taking care to favor sprinkling with all the weight of their sacred office.

Now, these things are true beyond contradiction; they are not fancies, but sober, sad facts, which I do not invent, but simply chronicle. If any man says I am impeaching the characters of good men, he is mistaken. I do not impeach them; but the facts—for which they alone are responsible, the facts of their own conduct—these impeach them. And I respectfully submit that Jesus himself impeaches them in these solemn words, "Why call ye me Lord, Lord, and do not the things that I say?"

On a certain Monday morning the pastors of the various churches in a certain city were chatting together freely in the Ministers' Association, when the Presbyterian minister introduced the subject of baptism by asking the Baptist minister whether he would be willing to immerse a member of the Presbyterian congregation, with the understanding that the person so immersed would become a member of the Presbyterian Church.

The Baptist minister, in reply, expressed a desire to be neighborly; but stated that he could not afford to take in washing; yet he would cheerfully lend his baptistery (the mill-race) to his Presbyterian brother, who could then baptize the candidate himself.

This brought on a general talk on the subject of baptism, when the Methodist Episcopal minister made this remarkable statement: "I have long noticed that when any one of our ministers undertakes to investigate this question of baptism, he is sure to come out a Baptist."

There you have it. Investigation makes men Baptists. Given an earnest man, intent on learning the bottom facts; let him enter upon a vigorous search for the truth, and the result is ever the same—he comes out a Baptist.

Evidently, then, those who are determined to persist in sprinkling—and in the sprinkling of infants—and to build up churches adhering to those practices, are obliged to discourage investigation. But this can not safely be done openly. If you tell an American he must not investigate this or that—no matter what—then he will surely arise and investigate that thing at all hazards. You have trenched upon his liberty, or challenged his curiosity, and he will let you know that he can investigate. No; that will never do. Open hostility to the investigation of this baptismal question would explode every pedobaptist church in America in ten years.

There is a better way. Treat it as a small matter; the average American despises small matters. Laugh at it as a ridiculous thing; the true American has a keen sense of the ridiculous. Turn away from it as a frivolous matter —as one who has far more urgent and earnest work to do; the typical American is an intensely earnest worker. Continually speak of it in terms of disparagement, as a thing of no importance whatever, an affair of no interest any way, and tell the people it is a matter of indifference to you how it goes. Do these things, and multitudes will say: "There, that's the talk. Who wants to waste time on little ridiculous, frivolous, indifferent matters?" Now, I say not one word of the motives of our pedobaptist leaders; but that in these last sentences I have faithfully portrayed their actual conduct in respect to baptism, and the evident effects of that conduct, no sane man, blest with two good eyes, two faithful ears, and an honest heart, will care to deny. And if any man does deny it, let him remember that facts are stubborn things; and that the facts that I have described abound in every community in this Christian land, and that they speak in a voice no man can drown, and tell a tale no man can disprove. And let him also remember that he who fights against the evidence of facts enters upon a hopeless task. He engages in a bootless struggle and wages a foolish war, in which his crushing defeat is only a question of time. In his case, prudence is the better part of valor. For him no valid defense is possible.

What, then, must be the motive underlying this policy of indifference? Is it, as many claim, a high degree of spirituality? But what sort of spirituality is it that ignores the words of Christ? What is the nature and source of that spirituality which scorns to inquire after the true sense of his words? How much of Christ is there in that spirituality which openly brands his own ordinance as a mere form? which jeers at it as a small thing? which pompously holds a faithful administration of it as a matter of ridicule? which boldly proclaims obedience to his word a matter of indifference? Is there one sane man who dare pretend that such spirituality is inspired by the Holy Spirit? Think you the Holy Spirit prompts men to cast contempt upon a command of Christ? I tell you, Nay. That spirituality which moves men to treat the word of Christ with indifference is not from above. The spirit that generates it is from beneath. The Holy Spirit takes the things of Christ and shows them to his people, that they may love them, honor them and do them. It prompts to obedience to Christ, to tender regard for his slightest wish. It is another spirit that leads men to hold up to ridicule a solemn ordinance, instituted by the express command of our Lord. It is a spirit far from holy that prompts men to treat that ordinance as a mere form, and its proper observance as a matter of indifference. "Try the spirits whether they are of God." A spirituality that pretends to pit love against obedience, that is too loving to obey, is simply a fraud. It comes not from heaven, but from earth and hell; and its essence is neither less nor more than an intense selfishness. These words may seem severe, and they may burn in some hearts, but they are true; and God give them pungency.

No; such spirituality as pleads for indifference to a command of Christ is not, and can not be genuine. It is a selfish counterfeit, and its great purpose is to shield an indefensible practice from an honest, searching investigation. It is the countersign of indifference, the only remaining citadel of those figments of popery—sprinkling and infant baptism. The moat around that citadel is the last ditch of pedobaptism, and the leaders know full well that it is their last line of defense. So long as men do not investigate, the cherished inventions of men are safe; but when they begin in real earnest to ask, "What is truth?" then the days of those idols are numbered.

Aye; there's the rub. Do not think for yourself, my pedobaptist friend. It is dangerous; for "*If you are determined to go to the bottom of this matter, you will come out a Baptist—there is no help for that.*"

NUMBER VIII.

" Well, that is the way all those German scholars write on baptism, but we think they are mistaken."

About six weeks after I began the study of baptism I received a most comforting letter from Rev. Mr. S——, a Presbyterian minister. He was a very dear friend, and having heard of my troubles he wrote me, expressing a profound sympathy with me in my search after truth. He said that, after all, my trials in respect to baptism were nothing new in the experience of pedobaptist ministers. He said that at some period of his ministry almost every one of our ministers encountered the same doubts which were now harassing me. He said he had passed through the same ordeal years before, and remembering his own sufferings at that time, he greatly desired to be of some service to me. He reminded me of the fact that he had a large library, much larger than mine; that he was much older than myself, and that he was, therefore, in a position to give me real, substantial aid in my investigation. He then earnestly invited me to visit him at his home, where we could go over the whole subject together, aided by the helps in his large collection of books. He also desired me, if I accepted his invitation, to send him immediately a brief statement of the points upon which I was in doubt, that he might review them and be the better prepared to aid me on my arrival. He closed by assuring me that he desired me to make my investigation thorough, and that if, as the result of it, I felt it my duty to go to the Baptists, I should go with the earnest prayers of himself and all the brethren for my prosperity, usefulness and happiness.

It was a noble letter, doing great honor to the heart and the head of the writer. I read it with great delight, and hastened to accept his generous invitation and proffered aid. I sent him a statement of the doubts besetting me, and named a time some weeks ahead, when I would visit him, should a kind Providence permit. The visit required a long journey—one hundred and fifty miles, mostly by private conveyance. But at the appointed time I started in high spirits, feeling sure of relief, and in due time arrived at the residence of my friend. It was a farm-house in a most beautiful valley; a lovely retreat.

The family gave me a hearty welcome and

immediately called my friend. He was in the field, superintending the labors of some workmen. Coming to the house, he greeted me with great warmth, making me feel entirely at home. It was about eleven o'clock of the forenoon, and he begged to be excused an hour, as his presence was needed in the field to give further directions to his men.

"After dinner," said he, "I will be at your service constantly, as long as you may need me."

Of course I excused him, but being anxious to improve every moment in study, and having been tendered the free run of his library, I begged him to name the best author on baptism, that I might study him until the dinner hour. In response to this request he assured me that the very best work in his library was Christian Knapp's "Systematic Theology." Entering the library I soon found the book, and turning to the article on baptism, I was instantly almost paralyzed with astonishment. For this great pedobaptist scholar and theologian began by affirming distinctly and positively all that the Baptists claim, and continued by proving the truth of those affirmations. In a word, his article on baptism is substantially the same as that of Storr and Flatt, which is quoted largely in another part of these sketches. To sum it all up, Christian Knapp assured me that the original baptism was the immersion of the body in water, and that the change to sprinkling is a matter of regret. And this is the best author in defense of sprinkling in the library! And what is the sum of his defense? Why, this—and this only —that a change has unfortunately been made, but that to set aside this invention of men and return to apostolic practice involves too much trouble. It was a plain confession that sprinkling has no warrant in the word of God; that it is, indeed, nothing less than rank disobedience to the command of Christ; but that, all things considered, it is better to continue to disobey the Master than to face the difficulties sure to arise among the brethren if we return to the practice of the baptism he commanded—immersion.

Presently my friend returned from the field. I met him at the door, greatly agitated, and at once told him what I had found in Christian Knapp. And this was his reply: "Well, that is the way all those German scholars write on baptism, but we think they are mistaken." If I was astonished before, I was fairly confounded now. This was help with a vengeance. How long, at this rate, would it take to vindicate the apostolic character of sprinkling? All the pedobaptist writers of Germany confessing it an invention of men! All of them agreeing that Christ enjoined immersion; that the apostles and primitive Church practiced it; that it continued the practice of the whole Church for many ages! All of them affirming that it was supplanted by sprinkling, not only without divine authority, but against the example and the plain, explicit command of Christ!

It is true that my friend had said, "We think they are mistaken." But had he not just indorsed Christian Knapp, one of these same German scholars, as the best authority on baptism in his library? What could it all mean?

I was greatly perplexed, but I decided to keep quiet and wait for further developments. I did not have long to wait. After dinner Mr. S—— informed me that on the receipt of my paper containing a statement of the points on which I was in doubt, he began to look into the matter, but very soon found that he had grown rusty on the whole subject, and that he could not do justice to it. He had, therefore, taken the liberty to hand my paper to Rev. J. H——, a Presbyterian minister residing in the next village, some two and a half miles distant. He informed me that Rev. J. H—— was a very venerable man—over seventy years of age; that he was also a man of very fine culture and fervent piety. He also assured me that he was thoroughly posted on the whole question of baptism, having just completed a full examination of it, to satisfy himself that he was really a baptized man. He also informed me that this was the third time since he entered the ministry that Rev. J. H—— had thoroughly investigated the whole matter to satisfy his own doubts, and that now he was fully satisfied and firmly established in the belief that sprinkling and infant baptism are right and entirely scriptural. He ended by requesting me to go with him to see Rev. J. H——, who was expecting me and would cheerfully render me all needed aid in searching for the truth.

I went with him and received an introduction to the aged and venerable gentleman. I found him a person of the most prepossessing appearance, a man of large stature, commanding presence, a fresh, ruddy countenance, penetrating eyes and snowy locks. I soon discovered that he was a fluent talker, and that he was very fond of talking. After a brief general conversation Mr. S—— departed, inviting me to return to his house in the evening.

Rev. J. H—— occupied an arm-chair in the middle of a very pleasant sitting-room, with his feet resting on a stool. I sat upon a hassock at his feet, and, looking up into his genial face, I said: "I come to you as a child comes to his father, seeking instruction. In me you have a willing pupil, anxious to be convinced that our practice respecting baptism is right and scriptural; but anxious above all things to find out the truth and do it, even though it should require great sacrifices at my hands."

In reply, he commended my desire for instruction in the truth and promised me the fullest satisfaction, telling me he had not a vestige of doubt that our views and practices were right, nor did he doubt his ability to convince me fully of their entire correctness.

He then launched into a general talk on the subject of sprinkling and the baptism of infants, continuing, without interruption, three hours and a half. He then stopped, saying he was weary, but if I would return the next day he would discuss the subject more fully. Thanking him for his kindness, and promising to call on him in the afternoon of the next day, I rose and returned to the residence of Rev. Mr. S——.

The next afternoon I called on Rev. J. H——, according to promise. At five o'clock I resumed my seat on the hassock at his feet, asking him to answer three questions, as soon as convenient, assuring him that if they were satisfactorily disposed of, I could get along with all other matters related to the subject, and remain cheerful and contented in the pedobaptist ranks. He agreed to reply to them directly, and resumed his talk.

At six o'clock I ventured to interrupt him, and remind him of his promise to reply to my questions.

He bade me be silent, saying I need not imagine he could not answer them; that he would do so presently.

He talked on until seven o'clock, without making any allusion to my questions, and then I ventured once more to call his attention to them, and to request some definite reply.

Somewhat impatiently he bade me keep still, that he would reply to my questions in a short time; and again I subsided, and he talked on.

At eight I again called his attention to the questions I had submitted, and which he had promised to answer, and earnestly besought him to gratify me by an immediate reply to them.

With great impatience he told me I must not presume to dictate to him, that he would answer my questions in a short time; but that meantime I must permit him to take his own way.

I bade him go on his own way, and assured him that I would not interrupt him again.

He then resumed his talk, talking on until half-past twelve o'clock, but without even attempting any reply to my questions. About twelve o'clock he gravely informed me that *baptizo* might properly enough be translated *to drown*.

That was a little too much for my self-control, and looking him firmly in the eye, I said:

"Are you willing, reverend sir, to risk your reputation as a scholar on that statement?"

"Well, no," said he, "you needn't take it so seriously. I was only half in earnest."

At half-past twelve he informed me that he had nothing more to say on the subject; that if I was not convinced by what he had already said, I probably could not be convinced at all, and ended by intimating a desire to know how his talk had impressed me.

I replied that the desire was a natural and proper one, which it would give me great pleasure to gratify.

"You have certainly proved yourself a fluent, shrewd talker," said I, "and have given evidence of a thorough acquaintance with the subject; and you have talked, in all, ten and one-half hours, but in all that time you have not produced one valid argument for your cause, not one argument worthy the name. You have dealt in witticisms, sophisms, evasions, and all manner of tricks, cute and sharp in many instances, but all of them too transparent to deceive a man of honest heart, open eyes, and an earnest purpose to find the truth.

"A cause which can not produce one sound argument in a talk of ten hours and a half by a champion so devoted and so eloquent, must be very weak and doubtful, indeed. I came here earnestly hoping to be convinced that our baptismal doctrines and practices are right; but your address has almost convinced me that they are wholly wrong, and that the much-abused Baptists are really in the right."

I had risen from my hassock, and was standing in front of him, looking at him with great earnestness, not unmingled with some degree of indignation at the manner in which he had trifled with me, for no man feels flattered at the discovery that another has endeavored to dupe him.

He was greatly excited and deeply angered by my plainness of speech, and replied with crushing severity:

"The Lord always knew there would be some people gotten up on a scale so narrow and bigoted that they could not be anything but Baptists, and so he instituted the Baptist Church for their benefit; and it is plain that you are one of that number, and so you will have to go and join them."

"Since you acknowledge that the Lord instituted the Baptist Church," I replied, "you will do well to be careful how you fight it."

This ended the discussion, and we went into his library and selected an armful of books on baptism, which I took home with me to examine, afterward returning them to him by express. I studied them very thoroughly, but it was of no use. The truth became every day more evident, and I was obliged to accept it, or prove myself false to my solemn vows, and false to my Lord. My Bible, honestly construed, was a Baptist Bible, and I could not make it countenance sprinkling or justify the baptism of unconscious babes.

I therefore tendered my resignation as pastor of the Congregational Church, assigning, as my reason for doing so, the decided change in my views respecting baptism. It was sorrowfully accepted, and I soon became identified with the Baptists.

Years have passed since then—years of constant Bible study, and of faithful, earnest toil in the Master's vineyard. They have brought with them varied experiences and great changes, and enlarged views of Bible truth and of Christian duty.

I am rapidly turning gray, and very soon men, judging by my whitened locks, will begin to call me old; but my Bible (Authorized Version of King James) is still a Baptist Bible. And I have long since learned that God owns his own ordinance, when administered in his own way, as he does not own the sprinkling of infants or of adults.

Those German pedobaptist scholars still continue to write in defense of immersion, as the real, original and scriptural baptism, and their example seems somewhat contagious, for French, and Scottish, and English and American pedobaptist writers are coming, more and more every year, to do the same thing.

And yet brethren, like my friend, Rev. Mr. S——, "*rusty*" brethren, are of the opinion that they are mistaken. And this is only too natural, for there is no other confidence quite so immovable as the confidence of willful ignorance.

Such *rusty* minds will continue rusty to the end, for they are entrenched in their own firm resolve to remain as they are. If you do not care to let in the sunlight, close the blinds, shut out the golden beams, and rejoice in the glimmer of a tallow taper; but know assuredly that the sun will flood the earth with light, clothe it with verdure and beauty, and fill it with life and loveliness, despite your tallow taper and your closed shutters.

Shutting out the light of truth does not pay any better than shutting out the light of the sun. It can have only one result. Sooner or later it must bring moral blight. God is the God of truth, and those who would be his must love the truth, and welcome it, and walk in the light of it. I accuse no man, but to me it is a strange thing that so many cling persistently to practices, in the name of the Lord, which are not required by his Word—nay, which are known, beyond any reasonable doubt, to be neither less nor more than the inventions of men.

Religious conservatism, within proper bounds, is a good thing; but when it prompts men to cherish error and reject the truth, it has become a foe to all true piety and Christian growth.

NUMBER IX.

"Why, sir, I am surprised to hear you speak in such terms of that book. It's a grand book, sir: a grand book. It has no equal. Its arguments are altogether unanswerable."

"Well, to be honest about it, I must confess I have not read the book myself. I formed my opinion of it from the testimony of others."

A MONTH or so after I began the earnest study of baptism, I called to see the pastor of the Congregational Church in a neighboring city. He was not at home, so I left word with his wife that I was in trouble, and that if he had any light on the subject of baptism, I desired him to let it shine for my benefit as soon as possible. In a few days he sent me a new work on the subject, from the pen of a celebrated divine, and I hailed it with great joy, for I had heard much about it, and I hoped to find in its pages the needed light and relief.

So I entered at once upon the study of it. At the outset, the author, with his characteristic candor, declared that all previous defenses of sprinkling were failures, and that if the classic sense of *baptizo* is to be accepted as the New Testament sense of it, there is an end of all discussion, and any defense of sprinkling is simply impossible, since the word in classic Greek always means to immerse. Hence, unless it can be shown that in the New Testament Greek it has another meaning, we might as well surrender at once, and confess that, after all, the Baptists are right.

But the author knew a better way than that. He had made a remarkable discovery—a discovery destined to overthrow the Baptists utterly, and settle the controversy forever. By some means he had found out a fact hitherto universally overlooked, namely, that, in the New Testament Greek, the word *baptizo*, with all its derivatives, is used in a sense altogether foreign to its meaning in the classic Greek; that, while in the latter the word always means *to immerse*, in the former it never means *to immerse*, but always means *to purify*.

Had I been less eager to find some sort of defense for sprinkling, the very audacity of the author might have put me on my guard. It would, doubtless, have seemed very strange that a fact so important had been so long overlooked by such a vast throng of earnest, able, critical students of the Bible. It would have seemed almost incredible that the hosts of lynx-eyed controversialists had for generations failed to notice a fact so vital, and so easily observed. Indeed, had I not been extremely anxious to find it true, I must have regarded it with suspicion, as in a high degree improbable; a statement to be labeled, "Important, if true," and to be received only when established by the most satisfactory evidence.

But I must confess that I hardly thought of these and correlated considerations. On the contrary, I swallowed the whole thing at once, rejoicing that at last I had found relief, and that I had got out of the current in which I had been drifting, and landed safe and sound on the pedobaptist shore. So, with a light heart, I plunged into the study of the book, not so much to discover the truth or falsity of the author's erroneous pretensions, as to learn the fact he asserted for myself, and to prepare myself successfully to assert and defend it. But, alas! for our plans, our hopes, our weaknesses! especially if they are pedobaptistic. A great poet says:

"The best laid plans o' mice and men
Gang aft agley,"

and I found his words even more truthful than poetic.

The book—a large one—was an utter failure. The writer said many beautiful things. The book was full of pen-pictures, entertaining, eloquent, pathetic, but destitute of argument. The grand postulate with which the writer opened so boldly was not proven. That was bad—a wet blanket to my fever of hope—but that was not the worst of it. Long-continued and searching study of the book convinced me that it was entirely false. The writer proposed to prove that the word *baptizo*, with all its derivatives, is used in the Scriptures in the sense of *to purify;* but instead of proving that, he proved that it is not so used. How shall I describe my disappointment, the deep humiliation and bitterness of it? I can not do it. It was crushing.

But, after a little, I gathered new courage to go through the book again, in the faint hope that I might yet find some different result. So I plodded through it again and again, only to be more firmly assured that the author had not only failed to establish his proposition, but had fairly proven exactly its opposite to be true. The Baptists could hardly desire a better vindication of their views than this book, the supreme effort of one of their most talented opponents.

I turned from it, almost sick at heart, yet not willing to confess myself vanquished. So I gathered about me the works of many other authors in defense of sprinkling and infant baptism, and continued my laborious investigation.

While thus engaged, Rev. G. S——, the Congregational pastor, who sent me the book which I had found such a painful, yet splendid failure, came to visit me, and aid me in my study. He was a lovely man, a very dear friend, and I gave him a most hearty welcome. Of course, our conversation was of the one theme which then so imperiously challenged my attention—baptism.

I showed him a letter from Rev. Mr. C——, the Presbyterian minister who, years before, had lectured me so vigorously and so successfully on the unscripturalness and destructive tendency of open communion—an incident elsewhere described in these sketches. He read the letter in great astonishment, for it was a lengthy and pathetic warning against the Baptists because of their offensive close communion. He who had so energetically pictured the wickedness and folly of open communion, and had so heartily supported and commended close communion as scriptural and wise, now bewailed my tendency toward the Baptists; not because their views of baptism were wrong, for that he did not affirm, but because of their "bigotry" in teaching and practicing the very same principles he had urged upon me, and which he himself had never ceased to defend and practice.

My friend could hardly believe the evidence of his senses, as he read that remarkable letter; but he knew the handwriting and style of the author too well to doubt the genuineness of it.

I proposed this question: "If close communion is scriptural and right for Presbyterians and Congregationalists, as our friend, Rev. Mr. C——, so eloquently maintains, and as we all believe and teach, how can it be unscriptural and wrong for Baptists?" My friend agreed with me that it was not fair to condemn in Baptists that which we approved as right in our own practice. And although he was a warm friend of Rev. Mr. C——, he did not hesitate to condemn his letter as an unmanly and unworthy attempt to influence me by an appeal to my prejudices.

I knew my friend was very anxious to learn what influence the book he sent me had exerted upon my mind; but I carefully refrained from any allusion to it, preferring that he should introduce the matter in his own way.

At length, as we were seated at the tea-table, he could wait no longer, but bluntly inquired what I thought of the book which he had forwarded to me.

I told him it was well written; that the author's style was lively and entertaining, and that no one could deny that the book was readable.

"But," said he, "what do you think of the argument? Isn't it convincing?"

"The argument!" I replied; "why, my dear sir, I didn't find any in the book. As I told you, the book is lively and entertaining, the language is very fine, and there are many eloquent passages in it; but there is no argument there—not a bit of it. As an argument, it is an utter failure; doing great discredit to its author."

"Why, sir," he replied, "I am surprised to hear you speak in such terms of that book. It's a grand book, sir—a grand book. It has no equal. Its arguments are altogether unanswerable."

Now I knew my friend had never read the book—at least, that particular copy of it—for when it came to me most of the leaves were uncut. So I quoted a passage from pages where I had cut the leaves, and inquired his opinion of that.

"Tell me candidly, my friend, do you think that a sound argument?"

"Well, no; there is no argument in that. But, surely, you did not find that in Dr. B.'s book, did you?"

"Yes, sir; I found it in his book, on pages so and so, just as I give it to you."

Then I proceeded to quote another passage from pages where I had cut the leaves, asking his opinion of that, and, as before, he responded by condemning it as altogether unsound, but suggesting a doubt whether it was really in the book. To this doubt I responded as before, naming the pages where he would find it. Then I named another passage, and another, and still another, each of which was disposed of in the same way; the evident embarrassment of my friend increasing rapidly meanwhile, until at last he could endure it no longer.

"Well," said he, "to be honest about it, I must confess I have not read the book myself. I formed my opinion of it from the testimony of others."

Then we reviewed the book together, and he heartily indorsed my opinion, that, as an argument, the book is an utter failure.

But my amiable friend was not discouraged by the evident failure of the book he had relied upon so ignorantly and yet so confidently. He entered into a general discussion of the subject, endeavoring to convince me that, after all, sprinkling is all right, as a social and climatic necessity, and our conversation continued until two o'clock in the morning.

He called my attention to the fact—which I could not deny—that baptism is only an outward form. But when I reminded him that back of that outward form is the command of Christ enjoining it, and inquired by what authority I could set aside his command, he had no reply to offer.

He assured me that sprinkling is much more convenient than immersion, and I was obliged to confess he was right about that. (To tell the whole truth about it, he had struck a tender spot, for one of the chief reasons why I so much dreaded to give up sprinkling and accept immersion was this very consideration of convenience. Immersion seemed an almost intolerable cross, from which I shrank with great dread day and night.)

But when I reminded him that Christ knew as much about the inconvenience of immersion as we did, and begged him to tell me whether the plea of inconvenience could be relied upon as a valid excuse for a neglect of duty, or for a disobedience to a command of Christ, he was silent.

When he urged the greater popularity of sprinkling, I was obliged to admit it; but when I inquired whether it would be safe to plead that popularity against the authority of Christ, he was again silent.

Indeed, he soon agreed with me, that while it would be pleasant, in this matter, to follow the multitude, it would be safer, and far more Christ-like, to obey the Master, and do as he commands.

He called my attention to the Arctic regions, and told me that immersion would not be possible there on account of the intense cold. I replied: First, that we do not live in the Arctic regions, and therefore we can not plead the climatic condition of those regions as an excuse for not doing our plain duty here; and, second, that the narratives of Arctic explorers contain accounts of persons getting into the water amid the ice-floes, and remaining there much longer than would be needful for immersion, and that without the slightest injury. He conceded that this answer ended the Arctic argument, and, as a candid Christian man, he gave it up.

He then called my attention to a certain Rev. Dr. B———. He said that the doctor was once a prosperous, honored Presbyterian minister, but he became troubled about baptism, and finally joined the Baptists, and that he had stood in the water so much, baptizing converts, that his lower limbs were paralyzed, and he was a helpless cripple.

"Well," said I, "if I could be assured of such success in my ministry—if God would only give me such a multitude of converts—I would not hesitate a moment longer, but go and join the Baptists at once, and suffer the loss of my limbs gladly."

"Ah!" said my friend, "it is of no use to talk. You are sure to become a Baptist. It is only a question of time. I bid you godspeed in doing whatever you may decide is your duty."

This ended our discussion; and the next day he returned home, and I returned to the study of the great question of duty.

My friend fell into an error only too common —commending a book he had not examined, and indorsing an argument he had not tested for himself. He formed his opinion from the testimony of others. It was not a wise method, as the event proved; but it was, and is, the method of multitudes. How few examine these matters for themselves! The pew looks to the minister; the minister looks to some great doctor; the doctor looks to the denomination, and writes as he best may in defense of its practice. And who constitute the denomination? Why, the pews and pulpits that are looking to the doctor for guidance and instruction.

And when the doctor has written his defense of the views and practice of his denomination, the word passes along down the line that it is a most triumphant vindication of the truth. A few read it, and the rest form their opinion of it from the testimony of others. This is neither an accusation, nor a caricature, but a plain statement of an undeniable, though not very complimentary, fact, in the history of Christian life and doctrine.

Nor are we to imagine it to be confined wholly to the various sects of pedobaptists. It is an evil not altogether unknown in Baptist circles. Far too many people are Baptists for no better reason than that their fathers were, or that some friends are--a very poor reason, indeed.

How much better were it to do as did the noble Bereans, search and see whether these things are so! It is the opinion of many good people that the Baptists are apt to give too much time and thought to these controverted questions. In some cases that may be true--very likely it is true here and there; but, as a rule, it is not true. The masses of Baptist people, and even of Baptist ministers, are not as well posted in these matters as they ought to be. If every Baptist were at all times ready to give a reason for the peculiarities of his faith and practice, the truths underlying them would speedily receive a far wider recognition than they now do, and the period of their ultimate conquest of the Christian world would thereby be greatly hastened. If they are worth contending for at all, they are worth contending for very earnestly. If it be not wrong to make them the basis of a separate organization, it is not wrong to study them thoroughly; and to propagate them vigorously and victoriously.

Some people seem to imagine that all churches are alike, that there are no real differences between them; and, doubtless, this is true of certain classes of churches. It is difficult to detect any important issue at stake between the various denominations of Presbyterians, or between the various kinds of Methodists, or between the Congregationalists and Presbyterians. And it is really a sad thing that brethren differing so slightly are yet so zealous to maintain separate organizations, with distinct and often antagonistic interests, often producing painful and scandalous collisions, and unseemly rivalries and antagonisms. What is this but to divide the Church of God needlessly? and what is such needless division but schism?

Some people tell us such divisions are a good thing; but Jesus does not agree with them, for he prays earnestly that his people may all be one. The apostles did not think so, for they vigorously denounce schismatics, and bid us reject them. Let no one be deceived. Those who maintain needless divisions in the body of Christ are schismatics, guilty of a very great offense against our Lord and his Church. And if Baptist Churches are not based upon and demanded by the divine Word, they are schismatics, and ought to disband.

But if their existence is required by that Word, then all other churches are schismatic, and ought to dissolve. Or, in more general terms, every denomination ought clearly to justify its own existence by the authority of the Word of God, or cease to exist. No man can deny this except by calling in question the authority of the divine Word; but, if it be true, then the faithful study of denominational peculiarities of doctrine and of practice, is a plain, imperative duty. It is not enough, in controverted matters, to consult one's neighbor, and form an opinion from the testimony of others. As honest Christian men, we are bound to search, and see, and know for ourselves.

NUMBER X.

"They are a wicked family, and they want the babe baptized because they imagine that will save it. What shall I do? If I go down there and baptize it, I shall only confirm them in their mistaken views respecting the saving efficacy of baptism; but if I do not go, I shall offend them, and that I can not afford to do, for they are rich."

"Well, I will walk down that way, and let Providence decide the matter for me."

WHILE I was investigating baptism, and after I had reached the conviction that, whatever might be true of sprinkling, I must wholly desist from the practice of infant baptism, I exchanged pulpits with the pastor of the Congregational Church in a neighboring city.

At the close of the morning service, Rev. Mr. R——, a Congregational minister, who had charge of an academy in that place, came to me, saying that he was in great doubt respecting duty in an urgent case, and desired advice.

He said he had received a message just before

the morning service began, from an Episcopal family in the city, informing him that the youngest member of the family, a dear little babe, had been fearfully scalded, and that they desired him to come and baptize it.

"And," said he, "I do not know what to do about it. What is your opinion as to my duty in the matter?"

"Well," I replied, "perhaps you will not think my advice of much value when I tell you that I have decided to baptize no more babes? I am fully convinced that the practice is wrong, and, of course, my advice is to decline to do anything about it."

"Oh, well," said he, "I believe in infant baptism, of course. I have no doubt about its propriety, as a rule, but this case is very peculiar. They are a wicked family, and they want the babe baptized because they imagine that will save it. What shall I do? If I go down there and baptize it, I shall only confirm them in their mistaken views of the saving efficacy of baptism; but if I do not go, I shall offend them, and that I can not afford to do, for they are rich."

I repeated my advice that he should decline to baptize the babe, assuring him that I deemed that the only safe course. But he was not willing to accept such radical counsel. He seemed altogether irresolute and unwilling to act in any direction, and notwithstanding the urgency of the case, he continued to discuss the matter in a rambling, desultory sort of way.

At last he intimated that the babe might possibly be out of its misery and beyond the need of baptism, and added, "Well, I will walk down that way, and let Providence decide the matter for me."

Accordingly he moved off in the direction of the afflicted home, which was over half a mile distant. I remained near the church door, looking at him with strange emotions. He seemed determined to give Providence plenty of time to decide the matter for him, walking quite as slowly as a healthy, able bodied man could walk on such a beautiful autumn day, and on such excellent pavement.

At length he disappeared around the bend in the street, and I returned to my stopping place, wondering what the issue would be, and pitying the bondage of my friend, and, it may be, inwardly rejoicing that I was about ready to renounce forever a practice of such doubtful character, by which a good man could be so hampered, and, as it were, compelled to walk a race against death—the slowest winning.

After the evening service my friend came to

me in excellent spirits. "Well, Bro. R——," said I, "how did Providence decide?"

"All right," he replied. "When I reached the house, the dear babe had just departed, and, of course, that settled the matter."

This incident made a deep impression on me; especially did these words of Mr. R—— impress me: "If I go down there and baptize it, I shall only confirm them in their mistaken views respecting the saving efficacy of baptism." Did not his going down there, under the circumstances, have precisely that effect? They could not know the mental protest under which he was acting. They knew nothing of his hesitation about the propriety of the baptism in that family. They were in ignorance respecting his delay in starting. They had not seen him loitering by the way, in the hope that on his arrival the babe might be at rest. All these things were unknown to them. He had, indeed, arrived too late, but for that he had apologized in apparent sorrow. His presence was evidence of his willingness to perform the service desired. It was also proof that, in his judgment, that service was both right and necessary. They had a right henceforth to quote his response to their request as an endorsement of their views of infant baptism, and he could challenge that right only by a confession, at once insulting to them, and damaging to his own reputation as a man of thorough integrity.

I do not doubt that he was afraid to baptize the babe, lest he might thereby confirm that wicked family in their mistaken views of the saving efficacy of infant baptism. But he lacked the manly decision and courage to take the only step by which he could escape such a result—a kind but firm denial of their request, and an honest statement of the true reason for it.

But hold. Let me not be too severe. It was not altogether a lack of courage. He was an advocate of infant baptism—a man of mature years and broad scholarship. How could he deny the saving efficacy of a practice, which, after all, can be defended on no other plea? Imagine him saying to that wicked family, "No, I can not baptize your babe. You think there is a saving efficacy in such baptism, but that is a great mistake. You rely upon baptism for salvation, but it can not save you. In it there is no saving virtue. If I were to baptize your babe, the baptism would do it no good. It is a mere idle ceremony, very pretty and sentimental, but of no real use. Under other circumstances it would give me pleasure to apply it to your babe, but you take it altogether too seriously. You think it really means something—that it will make your babe a partaker of the benefits of the covenant of grace, and thereby save it— that it is really circumcision in another form, and, therefore, necessary, lest your babe be cut off from all inheritance with God's people, and that it is essential to the putting away, or washing away the stains of original sin. I admit that we are continually affirming these very things, and many others like them, in our attempts to defend infant baptism from the assaults of the Baptists, but then we do not really believe them ourselves. I beg you, do not be offended with me. I am in a very difficult spot. I do not want to go back on infant baptism, for it is a very useful contrivance, by which such of our children as live to mature years are pre-empted, as it were, for our own churches, but otherwise it is of no value whatever. As I have said, you take it altogether too seriously, and rest upon it for salvation; and I dare not baptize your babe lest I encourage you in a delusion so deadly. I therefore beg you to excuse me from baptizing your babe, and please do not be offended with me, for I can not help myself; and, indeed, I desire your favor and patronage, for you are rich and influential."

Now that would be a very strange speech, I grant you, but for thousands of Protestant ministers who practice infant baptism it would be an honest speech, or at least as honest as the case would admit. But what would a "wicked family" be apt to say in reply?

It is often claimed by Baptist writers that every possible plea for infant baptism involves the idea of a saving efficacy in the rite, and it would be difficult for the most ardent friend of the "institution" to name a half dozen pleas in its behalf that are not fairly open to this charge. Indeed, our pedobaptist friends of the more evangelical denominations are sadly in want of some plea for the practice which clearly does not involve the idea of sacramental salvation. There is one such plea, as I happen to know. I never saw it in print, but having heard it urged by more than one intelligent, cultured pedobaptist minister, in defense of his own conduct in baptizing certain babes, I am very generously inclined to give all our pedobaptist friends the benefit of it.

Some years ago, while I was pastor of the Baptist Church in the city of M——, certain friends—members of the "Disciples" Church—came to me with certain well-founded complaints against pedobaptist ministers in our city; complaints valid against a large share of the ministers of pedobaptist churches everywhere.

At the next meeting of our Ministers' Association I said to the brethren: "Our 'Disciples' brethren have a grievance of considerable magnitude. They complain of your conduct, in a certain matter, as wanting in a manly consistency."

Instantly all were alert, two asking in the same breath:

"Why? What is it? What have we done?"

"Well," I replied, "they assure me that whenever a babe is likely to die unbaptized, you rush off and sprinkle it—an act which plainly says that you believe in the saving efficacy of it; but when they affirm that you believe baptism to be essential to salvation, you go back on your own actions and say you do not believe any such thing; and they complain that in this matter you are lacking in a manly consistency."

For a few moments there was an expressive silence in our midst; for several of the brethren had very recently sprinkled dying babes, and the facts were well known. The pastor of the Congregational Church was the first to break the solemn silence.

"Well," said he, "I might as well own up. Mrs. —— sent for me in great haste to baptize her babe, which was about to die, and I did it. Of course I knew there is no saving efficacy in baptism. I knew it would do the babe no good whatever; but the mother wanted it done, and I did it to please her." Then, after a moment's silence, he added: "Well, I am resolved that I will never do so again; never."

Then the pastor of the Methodist Episcopal Church said:

"I was sent for, not long ago, by Mrs. —— under similar circumstances, and I went and baptized the child. Of course I know as well as any one that there is no virtue in baptism to save the soul—not a bit of it—but I did it to please the parents."

Then another pastor made a similar explanation of his own conduct, giving the same plea, that "he did it to please the parents." Now I submit that this plea for infant baptism does not involve the idea of saving efficacy in it. On the contrary, it expressly discards all such notions. And it is certainly an amiable plea—"I did it to please the parents." A minister, no matter even if he were a Baptist, could not easily go farther in amiability than that. He knows the child, even in the presence of death, is just as well off without it; and it can do the little sufferer no good—"not a bit of it"—in any way; and he, poor man, may be fairly overrun with work; but he drops everything at once, and off he goes to baptize that dear little dying babe. Now, if it were an adult, a penitent believer, that called for baptism, other motives might induce even a very busy Baptist minister to drop everything else and administer the ordinance, even amid the snow and ice and the chilling blasts of midwinter. In fact, hundreds of Baptist ministers have gone out in the very worst weather to baptize people who were in no apparent danger of a speedy death. They have meekly stepped down into the freezing water, apparently surrounded by very many discomforts; but they did it only because God required it of them. I do not believe one of them would ever do it "just to please the parents" of the candidates, or to please any other friends. They are not amiable enough for that. In this peculiar kind of amiability our pedobaptist pastors excel. Not only do they often sprinkle babes "just to please the parents," but not infrequently they have been known to immerse people, and even such people as had been sprinkled in infancy, for the sole purpose of pleasing them. They certainly deserve their reward for an amiability so compliant.

Indeed, I think this plea, "I did it to please the parents," ought to be used a great deal more freely by pedobaptist ministers. The Baptists could not charge that it implies a saving efficacy

BEHIND THE SCENES. 141

in the rite. It is short and crisp as well as amiable. Everybody can understand it at once. It needs no labored explanation or learned defense. Then it is so definite in locating the authority in the matter with the parents, and in putting the responsibility upon them, that it leaves nothing more to be said. It classes infant baptism along with rattles, marbles and other toys, which one may or may not give to the child of his friend, just as the parent may fancy. Of course the parents must feel highly flattered. They are people to be "pleased." Here are grave and reverend pastors with no more sacred duty than just to *"please"* them. Here is a religious rite made entirely subservient to their pleasure. If they like it—all right. It shall be artistically arranged at their bidding; but if they do not like it, they need never have it in their houses. If they desire it for their little ones, it is a very beautiful Bible ordinance, which they can not prize too highly; but if they are prejudiced against it, they may spit upon it and kick it out of sight, for it is only a bit of the rubbish of old-time church usages, you know.

Here is flexibility for you; just the sort, too, that the pedobaptist pastor needs now in every community. Take any pedobaptist pastor you please, Presbyterian, Congregational or Methodist, and while some of the members revere infant baptism as a Bible ordinance, others of them can hardly endure it at all. Jones and his wife say: "It is a blessed thing. So sweet, so beautiful, so sacred!" And they have all the little Joneses duly christened; and when the dear pastor calls there, the talk is largely of this beautiful, sentimental rite, and of the "children of the church." But there is Bro. Miller. He abhors the whole thing, and his wife says: "No minister shall ever sprinkle a child of mine." And when the dear pastor ends his visit at the residence of Bro. Jones, and enters the home of Bro. Miller, he leaves infant baptism outside to take care of itself. Now, see how this plea helps him out. If he affirms that infant baptism is really a divine institution, he will feel obliged to defend it at Bro. Miller's and he will hardly fail to get into trouble; while Bro. Miller and his family, if he should become urgent in pressing them to obey it, will almost certainly go off and join the Baptists. But it is only a something to be done, or to be left undone, "to please the parents." So, at Bro. Jones', he pleases the parents by descanting upon its beauties; and at Bro. Miller's he pleases the parents, and indeed the whole family, by quietly ignoring it altogether. Sarcastic? No, sir. Simply true to the actual condition of things in thousands of pedobaptist churches to-day. If any man doubts it, let him open his eyes and look about him a little, and he will doubt it no longer. Demoralizing? Yes, but not more so than infant baptism itself. Not more so than any other defense of it. It does demoralize many men, but it also demoralizes infant baptism by degrading it into a mere bauble which intelligent and honest parents will soon learn to detest.

But no matter what may be the tendency, or the result of this plea, it is the only practicable one left to those devotees of infant baptism who, in their hearts, do honestly discard the figment of sacramental salvation. If they retain infant baptism at all, it must be simply as a mere matter of taste, or as a well-understood expedient to retain their hold upon the children and in due time draw them into the same fold with themselves. With these good people it is a time of transition and doubtful measures, but they are growing toward the truth and the light, and every year they become more evangelical, and in exactly the same ratio infant baptism declines among them. And the day is not far distant when they will cease to sprinkle babes, even "to please the parents."

NUMBER XI.

"How can a man write as this man does, and still continue to practice sprinkling?"

WHILE pastor of the Baptist Church in the village of O——, I received a call from the pastor of the Presbyterian Church, of a somewhat remarkable character.

He was a quiet, pleasant gentleman, rather cool and reserved in manner, and a little inclined to have his own way; but honorable and noble, generous and kind. In his way he was something of a philosopher, taking life pleasantly and smoothly. He used to say, laughingly, that "while it may be wicked to get angry, yet a little holy indignation is sometimes quite necessary." But in all our acquaintance I had never seen him indignant at anything, until that particular day already alluded to, when, to my great surprise, he was deeply agitated, and evidently very much offended. Without waiting to be seated, or even to remove his hat (he was usually a polite man), he cried: "Sir, I called to ask you a question, and I want a direct answer

—yes or no—and I will not be put off with anything else."

It was a beautiful day, a day that Italy might possibly equal, but certainly could not excel. The wonderful blue of the upper deep—cloudless and serene—seemed the very emblem of peace, itself a curtain vailing from mortal eyes the elysian fields just beyond. The earth reposed in a loveliness and beauty fairly entrancing. It was a day for reveries, for poetic visions and artistic dreams, and communings with Nature and Nature's God, amid the dim aisles of the grand old forests, God's earliest and holiest temples. But into the glowing harmonics of a scene so perfect, came crashing along this harsh, discordant note. What could it mean? Had a bolt of forked lightning and an earth-riving peal of thunder fallen that instant from mid-heaven, I could have been but slightly more startled and astonished. The shock staggered me for a moment, but presently "Richard was himself again," and I gently prevailed on my friend to be seated.

"Now, my dear brother," said I, when at last his hat was hanging gracefully on the rack, and he was settled nicely in my old study-chair; "now, my dear brother, ask as many questions as you please, and I pledge you an immediate, straight, categorical reply. I will say yes or no, or, I don't know, or whatever other word or words the nature of your question may require. Please say freely all you have it in your heart to say."

Looking me straight in the eye, and relaxing none of his firmness and fierceness of manner and tone, he replied:

"Sir, did you tell Elder W——, a few days ago, that Dr. Lange translates Christ's word, baptizing, by *immersing?* Did you tell him, sir, that Lange translates John's words (Matt. iii. 11), 'I indeed baptize you with water,' by the words, 'I indeed immerse you in water?'"

Returning his intense gaze with interest, I replied: "Yes, sir, I told Elder W—— all that, and more of the same sort."

"Why did you do it?" said he, his voice trembling with excitement.

"Because," I replied, "I thought he ought to know it."

"Now, sir," said he, "do you not know that Lange is a pedobaptist, a prominent divine and theologian in the Lutheran Church in Germany? Do you not know, sir, that he practices sprinkling?"

"Certainly," said I, "that is all true; no one doubts it."

"Yes," he replied, "no one doubts it; but how, then, dare you make such statements about him, as you confess you did make to a ruling elder of my church? How dare you say that he translates *baptizo* to *immerse?*"

"Why, sir," I answered, "I dared to say it because it is true."

"True!" he cried; "true! you surely do not mean to persist in your strange statement, after confessing that he practices sprinkling?"

"Why not," said I, "when it is true? As you claim, he does practice sprinkling, but he also translates *baptizo*, and its derivatives, to *immerse*, and thereby confesses that Christ has commanded him not to sprinkle but to immerse; and I have a right to state the fact—it is a public matter."

"I tell you," he replied, "there is some mistake about this. Your statement can not be true. Dr. Lange is a good man, and a great man, and he would never do a thing so absurd."

"Mr. K——," said I, "have you Dr. Lange's work on Matthew in your library?"

"Why, yes, I have it," he replied.

"Well, then," I rejoined, "why did you not examine it before coming here to accuse me of misrepresentation."

"Why, sir," said he, "I knew it could not

be true; and I could not believe you had really said so; and I thought, 'I will just run in and ask him about it, and that will settle it.' Of course, I might have looked into the book, as you say, but of what use would that be? Dr. Lange is a Lutheran. He practices sprinkling habitually, and it is not possible that he translates *baptizo* to *immerse*, for that would condemn his own practice."

I did not reply to this; but taking Dr. Lange's work on Matthew from a shelf just behind me, I opened to Matt. iii. 11, and, handing the book to Mr. K——, I bade him read for himself. Then, sitting down just in front of him, I watched his countenance as he read.

Poor fellow! I really pitied him. He grew red and pale by turns; and no wonder, for there he not only read, "I indeed *immerse you in* water," but, also, "He that cometh after me . . . shall *immerse you in* the Holy Ghost and in fire;" and then followed an elaborate explanation of immersion as the *symbol of a complete regeneration*, a change equivalent to a Death and a Resurrection, and all that from the pen of a great and good man, who, contrary to his own translation of the divine Word, was in the habit of sprinkling, instead of immersing, as the Lord commands.

At last my friend looked up, the very picture of astonishment, and in a bewildered but emphatic way, he said:

"How can a man write as this man does, and still continue to practice sprinkling?"

"Ah," said I, "that is the problem; but you see that I was correct, do you not? You concede that my statements about this matter were true, do you not?"

"Oh, yes," he replied, "your statements are true; and I most heartily confess the gross injustice I have so foolishly and unwittingly done you, and I earnestly beg your pardon for treating you as I did. I am very sorry for it, indeed."

"Say no more about that, my dear brother," I responded. "I most heartily and fully forgive you, and I sympathize with you most deeply in your feeling of pain at the gross inconsistency of those men who frankly confess that Jesus enjoins immersion, and then coolly keep right on sprinkling in his name. Do you know what Dr. Chalmers says about immersion?"

"No, sir; I do not recollect that I ever saw it," he replied.

I handed him "*Chalmers' Lectures on Romans,*" opened at page 152, at the beginning of his lecture on Romans vi. 3–7, and here is what he read from the pen of the greatest divine Scottish Presbyterianism ever produced:

"The original meaning of the word *baptism* is *immersion;* and though we regard it as a point of indifferency whether the ordinance so named be performed in this way or by sprinkling; yet we doubt not that the prevalent style of the administration in the apostles' days was by an actual submerging of the whole body under water. We advert to this for the purpose of throwing light on the analogy that is instituted in these verses. Jesus Christ by death underwent this sort of baptism, even immersion under the surface of the ground, whence he soon emerged again by his resurrection. We, by being baptized into his death, are conceived to have made a similar translation: in the act of descending under the water of baptism, to have resigned an old life; and, in the act of ascending, to emerge into a second or a new life, along the course of which it is our part to maintain a strenuous avoidance of that sin which as good as expunged the being that we had formerly, and a strenuous prosecution of that holiness which should begin with the first moment that we were ushered into our present being, and be perpetuated and make progress toward the perfection of full and ripened immortality."

As my friend read these grand words of the great preacher, he seemed deeply troubled. At length he closed the book, saying, as he did so:

"I can not understand it. How can a man write as these men do, and still continue to practice sprinkling?"

"Ah, my friend," I replied, "that is a very great mystery, but it is none the less a fact. If you will carefully look into the matter, you will find that nearly all of your great scholars, theologians and divines write substantially as these men write, and continue to practice substantially as these men practice. I will not accuse them; to his own Master must each of us answer. But there stands the fact, open, undeniable, and to me altogether unaccountable, that a great host of men—apparently wise and good men—continue through life in open, plain, constant disobedience to the command of Christ, themselves being the judges. For if I affirm solemnly, and as a public teacher, that Christ commands me to do a certain thing, and that his apostles habitually did that thing in obedience to his word, and that the doing of it inculcates the great, vital truths of Christianity—keeps them before the eye, as it were, in a solemn, religious tableau—and then I habitually refuse do what he has commanded, and, instead of doing that, do something else that he has not commanded, and do it, too, in his name, how can I deny that I am habitually disobeying him?

"I know full well the plea that these men urge in defense of their strange conduct—'that sprinkling will do just as well;' but how do they know it will do just as well? His own plain command is a sure proof that Jesus did not think that sprinkling would do as well as immersion. In his judgment, immersion is best—*is necessary to the end he has in view*—or he would not require it. Did not he know all about the greater convenience of sprinkling? Did not he know all about the rigors of a northern winter, and how necessary it would often be to cut the ice in order to immerse? Did not he know as much about the liability of ladies' clothing to float on the water as do the men of this generation, who so shamelessly urge it as an element of indecency?

"If he did not, then who is he more than another man? But if he did, then who are these 'great and good men' that sit in judgment on his command, and dare to condemn it as impracticable, or unwise, or in bad taste? Who are these doctors who presume to tell us that sprinkling, which Christ did not command, will do as well as immersion, which he did command?

Whence did they gain this wisdom, that they may correct the judgment of the Lord? By what authority do they set aside the authority of the Christ, and tell us that obedience to his command is a matter of *indifferency?*

"Why, *indifferency* to the command of an earthly king would justly be regarded as criminal - a fault to be swiftly and severely punished —and we are coolly told that it is a matter of indifferency whether we obey Christ.

"Who are these daring counselors, these bold innovators? 'Great men,' you say; wise men, educated men, good men—but men. However great, however wise, however educated, however good; they are, after all, men—only men.

"Then these men—themselves being judges — ask us to choose between men and Christ. They set the Word of Christ before us; they make it so plain that no room is left for doubt about what he requires, and then they modestly tell us in words, or by their own action, that they know a *better* way. And that brings us face to face with this simple yet awful problem: Which will we follow—Christ or these great men? Christ or these wise men? Christ or these learned men? Christ or these good men? Christ or men? This is the whole matter in a nutshell. Under which banner—Christ or men?

Choose ye this day. If you are Christ's, march under *his* banner, obey *his* command, submit to *his* judgment, keep *his* word, and be immersed simply because *he* commands it. But if you belong to these men, obey *them*—decide, if you dare, that obedience to Christ in the solemn act of confession of discipleship is a matter of indifferency, and please your own fancy. But be not astonished when you hear the sorrowful voice of your dishonored Lord asking of you that most uncomfortable question: 'Why call ye me Lord, Lord, and do not the things that I say?'

"I do not know, my brother, what you may think of this matter; but as for me, I prefer to follow Christ in this as in everything else, and that is the reason I became a Baptist. These men testify truly that the original baptism—the baptism which our Lord instituted, which he himself received in his own sacred person, and which he commanded us to receive and to practice—is an immersion of the body in water. This testimony is extorted from them by the force of resistless evidence—against all their denominational and churchly interests, and against their own evident personal tastes and preferences; and it is true, as a rigid, impartial examination never fails to demonstrate.

"And, my brother, every Christian man is shut up to this alternative—to obey Christ by being immersed, or to disobey him by accepting something else on the strange and daring plea that 'it will do just as well.'"

In a short time my reverend friend took his departure, a sad and thoughtful man.

Through a painful mistake he had made a very painful discovery—that there are professedly Christian men who concede that Christ does require immersion, and who still persist in the practice of sprinkling.

I do not wonder that he was surprised and grieved, and that he asked with such emphasis: "How can a man write as this man does, and still continue to practice sprinkling?" And yet the state of mind which enables men to do that is the sole defense of sprinkling and of infant baptism to-day. Let conscience assert itself in this matter, and put Christ on the throne—making his Word the word of a king in reality, a word to be heard reverently, and to be obeyed implicitly—and immersion instantly assumes its proper dignity as a gospel ordinance.

I said "conscience" advisedly; for it is the lack of conscience, in respect to this one matter, that keeps the practice of sprinkling afloat. Men do not intend to be disloyal to Christ in this thing; but they have drifted into a dangerous state, on the current of indifferency, lulled into false security by the force of great names, and the soothing murmur of a general assent. They fondly fancy the Master does not care, because he keeps silent, and utters no word of protest. If you chide them, they say, "Oh, it is only a form," forgetting that back of the form is the solemn command of our Lord enjoining it. Only a form, but a divinely-chosen form — a form enforced by the authority of Christ himself. When a Christian man is fully awake to this fact, he can not be satisfied with some other form than the one having divine approval.

It is idle to talk of it as "a mere question of water;" nay, worse, it is wicked to do so, because such pretensions raise a false issue and obscure the truth. It is a question of the kingly authority of Christ. It is a question of the supremacy of his law. There stands the law, plain, definite, explicit, positive, in full force. Only the same authority that enacted it can repeal it or in any way modify it, and that authority is silent respecting its repeal. The sacred lips that uttered the law of baptism have never, in any way, intimated even the slightest modification of it. How can a man ignore or disobey that law, and have a good conscience toward God? "Brethren, if our heart condemn us, God is greater than our heart, and knoweth all things."

NUMBER XII.

"*What can you plead in behalf of your dear children? You have rejected infant baptism, and with it the Covenant of Circumcision made with Abraham. What is there left? What can you now plead in behalf of your dear children?*"

"*Your question is a fair one. I have indeed rejected infant baptism, and as for circumcision, I have nothing to do with it. I am not a Jew, nor have I the least desire to be one. And yet I have one plea to urge in behalf of my dear children. It is a short, simple plea, yet one of infinite value. I can and I do plead in their behalf the blood of Christ, and I would not give up this plea for tens of thousands of Abrahams, and uncounted Covenants of Circumcision. I am satisfied with it.*"

SOME time after I had publicly renounced infant baptism and sprinkling, I received a letter from the wife of my former pastor. A descendant of the old Puritan stock, she was a lady of culture and refinement. A Christian of deep, fervent piety, she was also a zealous pedobaptist. With her, infant baptism was a very sacred and blessed institution, dating back to Abraham. In some way, to me unaccountable, she had come to associate it inseparably with the covenants of circumcision and of grace. It seemed to be with her a matter of early training and of reverent feeling, almost entirely. I do not think she ever examined it as a question of truth. I am confident she regarded it as a matter to be received and held by faith alone, and that she looked upon the intrusion of doubt respecting it as a visitation of the evil one, to be instantly, firmly and perpetually resisted and rejected, not by investigation and argument, but by prayer and a new resolution of faith and trust. An amusing incident in her quiet, earnest life will illustrate the great predominance of feeling over judgment in determining her conduct.

She was visiting a dear friend in a distant city, and while there (her friend being a member of the "Disciples" Church), much was said to her about the importance of submitting to baptism. Of course, she had been sprinkled in infancy, and she insisted firmly for a time that she was all right, while her friend assured her that she was really unbaptized, and therefore (in his opinion) unsaved. At length he said to her:

"You have long striven to follow the Savior, and to attain to eternal life. You have done many noble, Christly things—but you have not been baptized. You say it is not necessary in order to be saved. Perhaps you are right, but I think you are wrong. Now suppose you go on in this way until you come to the judgment, and then find that, after all, I am right, and that your sins are not forgiven; in a word, that you are lost. Would not a discovery of the fact, at that awful hour, be insupportable?

"Is it not vastly better to be on the safe side? Remember that, if I am wrong, I am still safe; but if you are wrong, you are lost."

She made no reply; but a few days after, hearing that there were to be several baptisms in the "Disciples" Church in the evening, she timidly inquired of her friend whether his pastor would baptize her, with the understanding that she should continue a member of the Congregational Church. Her friend replied in the affirmative, and then inquired whether she had changed her views.

"No," she replied, "I have not; but I have been thinking about what you said some days since about being on the right side. There is much in that, and I have resolved to run no needless risk; and therefore I desire to be duly immersed, and then I shall feel that I am certainly safe."

And immersed she was— though whether she went on her way any more joyously on that account, I can not say.

Of course my renunciation of pedobaptism was a matter of great mystery and great pain to her. She was a very warm, earnest, Christian friend, and she had reposed great confidence in me. When I announced my change of views, it was a great shock to her, although she had known for weeks that it was coming.

She could not easily become reconciled to it. After a time she wrote me a letter, very kind and very pathetic. In it she spoke freely of her great sorrow at the step I had taken; yet with the sincerest expressions of friendship and Christian affection.

She seemed to regard me as honest, but greatly deluded —as a wrong-doer, but not willfully so. In her view, I was rather the victim of misfortune than the blameworthy rejecter of divine truth. Her Christian charity did great honor to her heart, while her utter failure to grasp the great questions at issue, and to weigh fairly the reasons of my action, was not at all creditable to her head. And yet it was not the question of any lack of mental power, or of mental discipline, but of a vicious training which taught her to refer all questions touching religion to the heart rather than to the head; thus giving up to the guidance of blind feeling, in matters calling urgently for the undimmed gaze of the "eye of the mind"—the very mistake which, to-day, makes so many good men "blind leaders of the blind."

Referring to the fact that my children had been baptized in infancy, and that they were yet very young, she wrote:

"What can you plead in behalf of your dear children? You have rejected infant baptism, and with it the Covenant of Circumcision made with Abraham. What is there left? What can you now plead in behalf of your dear children?"

It really seemed as if she thought the salvation of my children depended on the Covenant of Circumcision; that in some inscrutable way their baptism had made them heirs of all its benefits, and that among those benefits the chief and crowning one is the salvation of the soul. In having them baptized, I, as their natural guardian, had really done no less than to place God under a solemn covenant obligation to save them; but alas! in renouncing infant baptism, I had released him from that covenant obligation. Having rejected infant baptism before my children were actually saved, I had forfeited all its benefits for them, and put them again outside the pale of the "covenanted mercies" of God. And if infant baptism is not a lie, and a cheat, she was right.

If there is any defense for it in the Word of God, that defense is in the plea of circumcision. Plainly there is no command, nor precept, nor example, in the Scriptures, enjoining or justifying it. The command to baptize is limited by the context to such as believe, as nearly all pedobaptists admit. Every precept, or principle, or illustration, in the divine Word, in any way touching baptism, relates, evidently, to the baptism of believers, and to such baptism only. And every example of baptism relates to the same class, and to them alone. The cases of household baptism are no exception to this statement, and furnish no pretense for the baptism of infants, since it is simply impossible to prove the existence of even one infant in any of those households, and in most of them the context makes it certain that all received instruction, believed in Christ, and rejoiced in him—things which infants are not in the habit of doing.

Glance at the cases of household baptism in

detail. We have no hint, not the slightest, that Lydia had either husband or children. The fact that she was a merchant, away from her own home (Acts xvi. 14, 15), renders it morally certain that she was unmarried, and the record of her conduct proves that she was a respectable, virtuous lady. Taking into consideration the known circumstances of her case, it is positively cruel to pretend there were infants in her family. If we were to assume as much about any respectable lady now living, we would call down upon us a speedy and very just prosecution for defamation of character. Dear old Sister Lydia can not defend herself in that way; but she is fairly entitled to better treatment at the hands of professed Christians, and I beg our pedobaptist friends, in the interest of Christian morals and decency, if for no other reason, to let her alone.

The members of her household are called brethren (Acts xvi. 40); but sprinkled babes are hardly brethren, those who sprinkle them being judges. Besides this, Paul and Silas "comforted" them (Acts xvi. 40). Were those noble missionary ministers itinerant baby-tenders? Did they talk baby-talk to one or more of those "brethren?" If I seem to talk foolishness, remember that I am replying to an unfounded foolish pretense, one that sensible and pious people ought to be ashamed to set up in defense of anything.

The jailer's household were not only baptized, all of them (Acts xvi. 33), but they were also taught, all of them, before baptism (Acts xvi. 32), and they all believed in God, all of them (Acts xvi. 34). To *that sort* of infant baptism Baptists will be the very last persons to object.

The household of Crispus were baptized by Paul (1 Cor. i. 14), but they were all believers (Acts xviii. 8). The household of Stephanas, which Paul also baptized (1 Cor. i. 16), were certainly believers, since they all became ministers directly afterward, and were so worthy of confidence that Paul directs the brethren at Corinth to submit themselves unto them—*i. e.*, to receive their instructions (1 Cor. xvi. 15, 16).

The household of Gaius may possibly have been baptized by the apostle, but as there is not the slightest evidence that they were, nor that Gaius had any household of any sort whatever, it would seem hardly safe to *assume* that he had a household, and in the household a babe, and that Paul baptized that babe, in order to find some shadow of excuse for infant baptism.

This whole matter of household baptisms does not afford even an honest pretext for infant baptism.

1. The presence of an infant is not necessary to the existence of a household. In my own congregation, at this moment, there are more than thirty well-regulated households without so much as one infant in any of them. And this word household is just as properly applied to these families that are destitute of babes, as to any others; and so it was anciently. Therefore, the word household of itself proves just nothing at all.

2. In every case of household baptism recorded in the New Testament, there is conclusive proof that the entire household were believers. These household baptisms, honestly studied, justify, not infant baptism, but the baptism of believers only. They are Baptist ammunition.

Nor can infant baptism be justified by the incident in the life of our Lord, recorded in Matt. xix. 13-15, Mark x. 13-16, and Luke xviii. 15-17, commonly described as Jesus blessing the little children. For Jesus did not baptize them, nor even hint that they ought to be baptized. His silence at such a time is conclusive proof that he does not desire their baptism. The passage shows beyond a doubt that Jesus is not a pedobaptist. It is the one grand incident in his life in which he is called to deal directly with little children as a class. He notices them, receives them, puts his hands on them, takes them up in his arms and blesses them, but does not utter one word about baptizing them; therefore, he did not intend they should be baptized.

This touching incident gives no countenance to infant baptism. It is also Baptist ammunition of the most effective sort, since it shows that Baptists, in neglecting the baptism of infants, are only following the undeniable example of our Lord.

There remains only one possibility of vindicating infant baptism from the Scriptures. If the Covenant of Circumcision is still in force, and if the form of the rite has been changed by divine direction into baptism; then the baptism of infants, under certain conditions, is an imperative duty. Is the Covenant of Circumcision still in force? and has the form of the rite been changed by divine direction into baptism? Suppose we look into this matter.

The Covenant of Circumcision was given to Abraham, and is recorded in Genesis, chapter XVII. It is in these words:

"1. And when Abram was ninety years old and nine, the Lord appeared to Abram, and said unto him, I *am* the Almighty God: walk before me, and be thou perfect.

"2. And I will make my covenant between

me and thee, and will multiply thee exceedingly.

"3. And Abram fell on his face: and God talked with him, saying,

"4. As for me, behold, my covenant is with thee, and thou shalt be a father of many nations.

"5. Neither shall thy name any more be called Abram; but thy name shall be Abraham: for a father of many nations have I made thee.

"6. And I will make thee exceeding fruitful, and I will make nations of thee, and kings shall come out of thee.

"7. And I will establish my covenant between me and thee, and thy seed after thee, in their generations, for an everlasting covenant, to be a God unto thee, and to thy seed after thee.

"8. And I will give unto thee, and to thy seed after thee, the land wherein thou art a stranger, all the land of Canaan, for an everlasting possession; and I will be their God.

"9. And God said unto Abraham, Thou shalt keep my covenant therefore, thou, and thy seed after thee, in their generations.

"10. This *is* my covenant, which ye shall keep between me and you, and thy seed after thee. Every man-child among you shall be circumcised.

"11. And ye shall circumcise the flesh of your

foreskin; and it shall be a token of the covenant betwixt me and you.

"12. And he that is eight days old shall be circumcised among you, every man-child in your generations; he that is born in the house, or bought with money of any stranger, which *is* not of thy seed.

"13. He that is born in thy house, and he that is bought with thy money, must needs be circumcised; and my covenant shall be in your flesh for an everlasting covenant.

"14. And the uncircumcised man-child, whose flesh of his foreskin is not circumcised, that soul shall be cut off from his people; he hath broken my covenant."

In the last five verses we have Abraham's idea of his part of this covenant in his method of applying it:

"23. And Abraham took Ishmael his son, and all that were born in his house, and all that were bought with his money, every male among the men of Abraham's house, and circumcised the flesh of their foreskin, in the self-same day, as God had said unto him.

"24. And Abraham was ninety years old and nine, when he was circumcised in the flesh of his foreskin.

"25. And Ishmael his son was thirteen years

old when he was circumcised in the flesh of his foreskin.

"26. In the selfsame day was Abraham circumcised, and Ishmael his son;

"27. And all the men of his house, born in the house, and bought with money of the stranger, were circumcised with him."

Is this Covenant of Circumcision still in force? This is not a new question. It arose at Antioch in the days of the apostles, and troubled the brethren there greatly. For certain men went there from Judea, and taught the people: "Except ye be circumcised after the manner of Moses, ye can not be saved." Paul and Barnabas contradicted them, but they insisted upon it, and the church was in a great commotion about it. At last, to set the matter at rest, they sent a committee, headed by Paul and Barnabas, to Jerusalem, to consult the apostles and elders about it. After a very earnest consultation, the apostles and elders decided unanimously that circumcision was not necessary, and they sent chosen men, Judas and Silas, with Paul and Barnabas, to tell the brethren at Antioch, in substance, that they need not be circumcised. Read the fifteenth chapter of Acts, and you will see that this first great Council of the Church, under the direction and by the advice of the inspired apostles, set aside circumcision as a matter not binding on the Church of Christ.

It is true, they expressed themselves very cautiously, for they were in great danger of exciting a deadly persecution against themselves, surrounded as they were by zealous Jews; but their letter to the church at Antioch is sufficiently explicit.

The refusal to enforce circumcision upon the church at Antioch was a deliberate, intentional notice to them, and to Christians everywhere, that it is not an institution of Christianity. I affirm, therefore, by the authority of the apostles of our Lord, that the Covenant of Circumcision is not in force among Christians.

Paul, in his letter to the Galatians, denounces circumcision as opposed to the gospel. (Gal. v. 2.) "Behold, I Paul say unto you, that, if ye be circumcised, Christ shall profit you nothing." And in the eleventh verse of the same chapter he says: "And I, brethren, if I yet preach circumcision, why do I yet suffer persecution? then is the offense of the cross ceased."

If circumcision is still in force, why did not Paul preach it? If it is a part of Christianity, why did he say, "If ye be circumcised, Christ shall profit you nothing?" If circumcision is still in force, then Paul did not know it, or he is a deceiver.

But it is said the form of circumcision is changed to baptism. But if this be true, why did not the Council at Jerusalem tell the brethren at Antioch that they were already circumcised by baptism? If it be true, why did not Paul tell the brethren of Galatia that they were already circumcised by baptism? If it be true, why were any baptized who had been circumcised?

If it be true, then all who are baptized are thereby circumcised, and Christ profits them nothing, since Paul says (Gal. v. 2), "If ye be circumcised, Christ shall profit you nothing." If it be true, then all baptized persons, being thereby circumcised, are bound to do the whole law, Paul being judge, for he says (Gal. v. 3), "For I testify again to every man that is circumcised, that he is a debtor to do the whole law." If it be true then, every baptized person, being thereby circumcised, is fallen into endless troubles and contradictions.

For, being circumcised, he has become a Jew, and as such he is an heir with them of the earthly Canaan, and he is subject, with them, to all the laws and ordinances of the Theocracy. Having become a circumcised man by baptism, in the very act by which he intended, solemnly and publicly, to "put on Christ," and avow himself a Christian, he has unwittingly "put on Moses"—and henceforth Christ avails him nothing; while, in addition to his own crushing burden of personal guilt, as a wretched sinner, he comes in for his share of the curse resting upon the Jews for their rejection of our Lord. At the same time, being by his circumcision "a debtor to do the whole law" (Gal. v. 3), he has no other way of justification open to him than by the law, and he is, therefore, fallen from grace. (Gal. v. 4). But by the law salvation is impossible, for "By the deeds of the law there shall no flesh be justified in his sight: for by the law is the knowledge of sin." (Rom. iii. 20).

Absurd? Yes—but the legitimate and inevitable result of this absurd notion that circumcision is still in force in the form of baptism.

No, circumcision is not in force. Christ abolished it: "Blotting out the handwriting of ordinances that was against us, which was contrary to us, and took it out of the way, nailing it to his cross." (Col. ii. 14.) And the Council at Jerusalem quietly dropped it as a thing no longer binding—an action the more significant from the fact that it was advocated by such inspired Jews as Paul and Peter and James, and was approved by all the apostles and elders, the most of whom were certainly Jews.

And Paul, the great apostle to the Gentiles, did not preach it, but constantly warned the Christian brethren to let it alone—telling them, in effect, that they could not have both Christ and circumcision; that if they were circumcised they would thereby forfeit Christ, and henceforth he would profit them nothing. And yet, in the vain hope of justifying infant baptism, men claiming to be Christians tell us that, after all, circumcision is not nailed to the cross; is not opposed to Christ; is not abolished, but is still in full force, in the form of baptism. When asked to name the chapter and verse wherein this change of form is authorized, they are silent. When called upon to vindicate the conduct of the apostles and elders in the Council of Jerusalem, they are dumb. When requested to explain how it is that Paul—who, according to their statements, was all the time preaching, and, at least sometimes, practicing circumcision—could honestly denounce circumcision, and affirm defiantly that he did not preach it, they are speechless.

When we inquire how it happened that the existence of circumcision, under the form of baptism, escaped the notice of the entire Christian world until so recently, they ought to blush with modest worth, but they suddenly become wonderfully deaf, and of course attempt no reply.

The truth is, this whole pretended argument for infant baptism from circumcision is an afterthought—a contrivance cooked up to meet a desperate emergency. Its weakness is exceeded only by its audacity, unscripturalness and endless inconsistencies. Its existence is a reflection on the piety of modern times, while the fact that any considerable number of men continue to employ it as a defense of the practice of infant baptism is a severe impeachment of the intelligence of Christendom in this progressive age.

Circumcision was a strictly Jewish rite. It began with Abraham and ended with Moses. It did not begin with the Dispensation of Promise. It was injected into that dispensation at a certain time, as a surety and means of the fulfillment of those temporal promises which were to prepare the way for Christ.

There was no Christ in circumcision, but it was designed and fitted to become the bond of a new national life, through which in due time he might appear. Abraham saw in it the beginning of the fulfillment of the long-deferred promises of future temporal greatness. It was to him an explicit, visible pledge of a numerous and powerful posterity, and for this reason it was to him a seal, or confirmation, of the faith and confidence in the promises of God which he had cherished so long and so patiently. This was its only connection with faith. Abraham saw in it an earnest of the realization of his long-deferred hope and trust. It was, therefore, to him a seal of his faith; but he received it, not because he was a saint, but because he was to become the Father of many nations, and especially of that particular nation through whom the Messiah should come. And his sons and his slaves and the sons of his slaves received it, not because they had faith, or were by and by to have it, but solely because they were his sons, or his slaves, or the sons of his sons, or the sons of his slaves, and, therefore, citizens of that new nation of which God had constituted him the founder and the head. They were entitled to it, not by faith, present or prospective, but by natural birth in the nation, in which it was the badge of citizenship. As a Jewish rite, it had its uses as a pledge or token of certain great temporal rights and privileges; but when Judaism gave place to Christianity, it was abolished along with the nationality of which it was the bond and the badge, and the Covenant of Works, of which it had also become the recognized bond.

Some, indeed, imagine that it still survives under the form of baptism. But if so, it has undergone a most complete and wonderful transformation—such a transformation as utterly destroys its identity, and converts it into a something in every way unlike its own former self, and in everything fatally opposed to it.

As to outward form, what can be more unlike than circumcision and baptism—the one a bloody cutting, the other a bloodless bathing?

As a religious type or symbol, while it is not opposed in signification to baptism, it is almost immeasurably inferior to it.

It symbolizes a putting off the sins of the flesh—a circumcision of the heart—but it does not even hint of the means of that circumcision, nor does it intimate the completeness of it. It indicates a lopping off of old evils—a partial reform in life—but it gives no promise of a new life, a divine life, charged to overflowing with good.

But not so baptism. That tells in its very form, not only of a cleansing, but of a change radical as death, and vitalizing as the resurrection. It symbolizes, not a mere lopping off of rotten limbs, but a dying to the old life of sin and a rising into a new life of holiness; and all this through the death and resurrection of our Lord. The one voices the demand of the law, the other describes, in eloquent action, the amazing victory of the Cross. The one is a "yoke of bondage," making those who receive it debtors to do the whole law; the other is a badge of liberty and life, assuring all observers that all who rightly receive it have passed from the bondage and death of law into the freedom and light and life of the gospel.

The one is the badge of citizenship in a temporal kingdom, and attests only a natural birth into a certain temporal nationality; the other is the badge of citizenship in a spiritual kingdom, and attests a spiritual birth into the kingdom of God.

The one belongs to the Covenant of Law, which says, "This do and live;" the other belongs to the Covenant of Grace, which says, "Believe and live."

The one is the natural birthright of all the male children of a certain nation, and of all their male servants and proselytes, no matter what their moral character; the other is the spiritual birthright of such, and only such, as are born of God, male or female.

The one is the token and badge of the Judaism whose letter killeth; the other is the token and badge of that Christianity whose spirit giveth life.

In a word, circumcision and baptism are as unlike in all respects as law and grace, as Moses and Christ, as Sinai and the Cross, as bondage and liberty, as death and life. They are not, they can not be, one and the same.

Baptism is not circumcision in disguise, but the new, divine, gospel rite, ordained by infinite wisdom as a perpetual and complete epitome of the central, vitalizing truths of the gospel of Christ; and, as such, it has nothing in common with Judaism, or its antiquated and bloody ceremonial rites. It comes to us, fresh from the heart and the lips of Christ, eloquent with his spirit and with his truth.

But Paul says (Col. ii. 11): "In whom also ye are circumcised with the circumcision, made without hands, in putting off the body of the sins of the flesh by the circumcision of Christ."

"Does he not mean that we were, in some way, thus circumcised in the person of the infant Christ?" Nay. The circumcision here spoken of is evidently that work of grace which he wrought in their hearts by his spirit—a work of which circumcision proper was only an imperfect symbol, and not that work wrought in his flesh when he was circumcised on the eighth day. That fleshly circumcision was made with hands, but this without hands. That put off a bit of the flesh of a sinless man, but this "puts off the body of the sins of the flesh" for sinful men. That was a carnal ordinance, this is a spiritual renewal. That was an act of obedience to the letter of the law, this is an effect of the operation of divine grace. That was a characteristic of the dispensation of types and shadows, this is the crowning glory of the dispensation of spiritual realities. That simply certified that Jesus was a Jew, and, as such, entitled to all the rights and immunities of a Jew; this made those Colossians genuine Christians, heirs and trophies of the regenerating grace of God.

But we are told that circumcision still survives in baptism, the latter being the badge of membership in the church now, as circumcision was anciently. This information would be very important, indeed, if it were true. It assumes the identity of the Christian Church and the Jewish Commonwealth—an assumption not only not true, but utterly and hopelessly false, in every particular.

The ancient Jewish Commonwealth was simply a religious nationality—a nation under theocratic government. The Christian Church is a spiritual body, having properly no political or national character or functions.

Take the Apostolic Church at Jerusalem and contrast it with the Jewish Commonwealth:

The one was composed of natural men, the other of regenerate men. In the one piety was not necessary in order to membership, in the other it was the chief qualification.

To the one were added daily by natural birth all male children of Jewish parents, to the other were added daily by spiritual birth such only as were saved. The one was made up chiefly of worldly, impenitent persons, with whom religion was an affair of forms and ceremonies and statecraft; the other was composed chiefly, if not entirely, of persons with whom religion was a matter of heart and life—persons who gave evidence of genuine penitence and living faith, and who willingly gave up all for Christ.

The members of the one boasted the law of God written on tables of stone, but ignored it in their lives. The members of the other had that law written on their hearts, and illustrated it in their lives.

The one institution was built on the Covenant of Works: "This do, and thou shalt live;" the other was erected on a better covenant, the Covenant of Grace: "Believe on the Lord Jesus

Christ, and thou shalt be saved." The one had the Levitical priesthood, with Aaron at its head; the other had but one priest, Jesus the Son of God.

The contrast could not well be more complete. The Christian Church is a new institution, distinct from the old Jewish economy, and totally different from it in all things; having a new and better covenant, a new and better sacrifice, a new and better high priest, new and better promises, a spiritual membership, admitted on new and better conditions, and by new and better tests of fitness.

If a man could demonstrate that black is white, that darkness is light, that evil is good, that sickness is health, that death is life; then, perchance, he might be able to prove that the old Jewish Commonwealth and the Church of Christ are one and the same.

They are not the same in any just sense whatever. They have not the oneness of identity, nor of continuity, nor yet of similarity. They have only the same God, and a part of his oracles of divine truth in common. And being so entirely unlike in all else, they are also wholly unlike in their badges of membership.

But suppose, for a moment, that the ancient Jewish Commonwealth and the Church of Christ are really one, and that circumcision does survive in the form of baptism, and that children ought to be admitted into this Jewish Christian Church now by baptism, as they were anciently admitted into the Jewish Commonwealth by circumcision. Admit all this and what follows? Why, nothing less than this: The Church must have a High Priest in its earthly sanctuary, as anciently. It must have its priests and Levites. It must have its heads of tribes, its Sanhedrim, and its voice of authority which none may dispute. And when it has all these things, what is it but the Church of Rome? And if this plea for infant baptism from circumcision is valid at all, it proves that the Church of Rome is the true apostolic, Jewish Church of Christ, and that all other churches are schismatic, heretical sects. And this puts Luther and Calvin, Knox, Cranmer and Wesley into a most unpleasant plight. For it exhibits them as most unsaintly schismatics, opposing the Pope and the true Church.

When our Protestant brethren have succeeded in proving the identity of the Jewish Commonwealth and the Church of Christ, their first duty will be to cease their protest against Rome, and to seek immediate reconciliation with her as the only true Church.

But I submit that an argument which involves

the inevitable overthrow of Protestantism is presumptively false, and ought not to be received by sincere Protestants, except as the result of the most careful scrutiny, and in obedience to the most rigid and undeniable proofs of its absolute truthfulness. If this circumcision-baptism theory could be proven, it would not only sustain infant baptism, but the Pope, the College of Cardinals and the entire machinery of Romanism. If true, it is the death-knell of Protestantism.

Protestant ministers engaged in the vain attempt to substantiate it could not possibly do anything more absurd and hopeless, nor can the wisest friend of Romanism devise a scheme more perfectly adapted to destroy the last vestiges of Protestantism and to give Rome universal and perpetual dominion. The only safety of the Protestant, and the only despair of the Romanist, is in the utter absence of proof of this theory nay, the presence of undeniable, overwhelming evidence that this entire claim of identity is false.

But, again, suppose we concede for a moment all that the most ardent devotee of infant baptism will claim, that the Covenant of Circumcision is now in force in the Church of Christ; that this covenant includes the Covenant of Grace ("In thee shall all the families of the earth be blessed."—Gen. xii. 3), and that the form of circumcision has been changed into baptism. Then these are some of the consequences that inevitably follow:

I. Male servants and slaves must be baptized, for such were circumcised.

II. Females must not be baptized, since they were not circumcised.

III. All the male children of members of the Church must be baptized on the eighth day, for that is the day named in the covenant.

IV. All males who are thus baptized are to be reckoned as the natural descendants of Abraham, entitled to all the privileges and bound by all the obligations of Judaism.

V. There are now no Jews in the world, except such as are baptized, since circumcision is performed now by baptism.

VI. The Church of Christ, and that alone, is the true owner of the earthly Canaan.

VII. All who are not baptized are forever lost, for the male child which was not circumcised was to be cut off from his people. He had no right to the benefits of that covenant, and if that was the Covenant of Grace, he was forever lost. If, therefore, baptism is the new form of circumcision, then no unbaptized person can have the benefits of the Covenant of Circumcision; and if that covenant be really the Covenant of Grace, then it follows beyond a peradventure that no unbaptized person can be saved.

Thus this boasted circumcision argument carries with it such consequences as demonstrate to every sane mind its utter falsity.

Do you wonder that I replied to the appeal of my old pastor's wife in terms indicating little respect for the Abrahamic Covenant of Circumcision as a warrant for infant baptism? That covenant was a good thing in its day. It served its purpose admirably, and then it gave place to a better and bloodless covenant—resting on the one offering of Christ, and assuring spiritual and eternal blessings.

God's Covenant of Grace made with Abraham twenty-four years before the Covenant of Circumcision, I did not and do not reject. That was confirmed in Christ by the very same act by which the Covenant of Circumcision was taken away and nailed to his cross. That Covenant of Grace is open to all. Baptism can not secure its benefits, nor can the lack of baptism forfeit them. If it were otherwise, then baptism would have power to save, and the absence of baptism would render salvation impossible.

But some tell us that Christians are children

of Abraham—that they are called the seed of Abraham. Yes, but in what sense? Not in the sense of natural generation, surely! No one believes a thing so ridiculously absurd as that! What then? Why, in a spiritual sense only. Abraham believed God—and his faith became an eminent example and illustration of all true faith. So he is called, by way of eminence, the father of the faithful. If then you believe God, you are a child of Abraham—in the sense that you do as he did. You follow his example. You become, by your faith, a member of the great company of believers, of which, because of the priority and eminence of his faith, Abraham has been called the father, and in that sense, and in that alone, are you his seed.

Does it follow that your child, born of your flesh, is of the seed of Abraham? By no means. Your child can become a child of Abraham only in the same sense, and in the same way, that you did—by believing God for himself. This is as plain as that two and two make four; and yet pious pedobaptist ministers are often conveniently blind to it. But a man who refuses to see it, ought not to wonder if men doubt his intelligence or the purity of his motives; they can not help it, and generally, as the more charitable way, they will give him credit for honesty at the expense of his judgment and good sense.

Being yourself a child of Abraham by faith, it is your privilege and your duty to endeavor by a holy life, by faithful instruction, and by earnest prayer, to induce your children to exercise a like faith, and to become thereby heirs with you of the heavenly inheritance. It is your privilege and your duty to do all you can to bring your dear ones to God, but you can do it only by way of the cross. The way to heaven is not by infant baptism, but by way of Christ crucified. Go with your dear ones to Gethsemane, and Calvary, and Olivet. Show them the dear Master agonizing and dying for their sins, and ascending to the Father; and if that does not bring them to penitence, and faith, and hope, you may rest assured that the baptismal font is of no use. If they will not heed the dying, risen Savior, you may depend upon it, they will not care for Abraham, nor for any or all of his covenants.

And when you carry their case to the throne of mercy, your weary, aching heart will need no other plea than the blood of Jesus. Indeed, that is the only plea that can find admission there. The devout Catholic may plead the name of the Virgin Mary there, but it can not be heard. The devout pedobaptist may plead the name of Abraham, but all in vain. Only one name can avail there—the name of Jesus. "If ye shall ask anything in my name, I will do it." That is a full warrant for claiming all you need, and it is from the lips of our Lord himself. All power in heaven and on earth is in his hands, and he is able to redeem every promise with absolute certainty. Bring your dear ones, then, in the arms of faith, not to the baptismal font, on doubtful authority at the best—on a supposed authority that has never yet been clearly vindicated, and that apparently never can be—but directly to Christ, and plead his own precious promise. In this you will be doing right beyond any doubt—for Christ himself invites you to do so in these blessed words: "Ask and receive, that your joy may be full," and "Ask, and it shall be given unto you."

Many years have passed since I received the letter from my dear old pastor's wife, asking me so pathetically, "What can you plead in behalf of your dear children? You have rejected infant baptism, and with it the Covenant of Circumcision made with Abraham. What is there left? What can you now plead in behalf of your dear children?" and I am only the more firmly convinced each passing year, that Christ is still left me, and that his name and his blood are an all-sufficient plea, and I still adhere to my reply: "Your question is a fair one. I have indeed rejected infant baptism, and as for circumcision, I have nothing to do with it. I am not a Jew, nor have I the least desire to be one. And yet I have one plea to urge in behalf of my dear children. It is a short and simple plea, yet one of infinite value. I can and I do plead in their behalf the blood of Jesus, and I would not give up this plea for tens of thousands of Abrahams, and uncounted Covenants of Circumcision. I am satisfied with it."

NUMBER XIII.

"I like the Baptists very much. They are a good people. But there is one thing about them that I never could understand, and that is their close communion. I can not see why they should be so narrow."

WHILE pastor of the Baptist Church in the city of P——, I formed the acquaintance of Sister M——, a most excellent Christian lady, a member of the Presbyterian Church. She was an elderly lady—a mother in Israel—always interested in every good work, and very fond of Christian conversation. She was too infirm to go abroad much, and at her request, I often called at her house to talk over the interests of the Master's work, especially in our city.

One day she surprised me by alluding to our denominational differences, a matter which had never before been mentioned in our interviews. After speaking of the zeal of certain members of my church in the cause of temperance, she continued:

"I like the Baptists very much. They are a

good people. But there is one thing about them I never could understand, and that is their close communion. I can not see why they should be so narrow."

Thus challenged, I thought it my duty to aid her in the solution of this very strange problem, so troublesome to so many of the dear disciples of the Master. So I said:

"Do you really desire to understand our close communion?"

"Certainly I do."

"Well, I think I can make it plain to you in a few moments."

"If you can, I wish you would. It would be a great relief to me to know that they have a good reason for it."

"Very well, I will try. You are a Presbyterian, I believe, are you not?"

"Yes, sir; I have been a member of the Presbyterian Church from childhood."

"Do you fully indorse the doctrines and usages of the Presbyterian Church?"

"Certainly, sir; I am a thorough Presbyterian, in all respects."

"Then you believe in the Presbyterian views and usages respecting the Lord's Supper?"

"Of course; I think they are scriptural and right."

"Well, let us see if we understand those views and usages alike. Presbyterians believe and teach that the Lord's Supper is a Church ordinance, and that only those who are members of the Church in good standing are entitled to partake of it. They also believe and teach that baptized persons only are members in good standing in any gospel Church. In other words, Presbyterians hold that only such persons have a right to that table as are members, baptized members, of evangelical churches, and they invite such and such only. Am I correct in this statement of their views and practice?"

"Yes, sir; you have stated our views and practice precisely."

"And you believe them fully?"

"I do; I have no doubt that they are scriptural and true."

"Then, if I am not mistaken, you believe firmly that scriptural baptism and church-membership are prerequisites to the Lord's table; that faith is not enough to entitle any one to appear there; and in this view you agree with the membership of the Presbyterian Church?"

"You are not mistaken. That is just what we believe and practice. We all think that a person who is not baptized, and who is not also a member in good standing in some evangelical church, ought not to go to the Lord's table. He ought first to be baptized and unite with some church, and then take the Supper."

"Exactly. And you think that those who are sprinkled are baptized, and therefore you invite them."

"To be sure we do. We accept sprinkling as valid baptism, and we regard infant sprinkling, too, as real baptism; but we do not reject immersion as baptism. We regard you Baptists as baptized believers, and would welcome you to the Lord's table among us. Why do you not welcome us to the Lord's table in your churches?"

"Ah! that's the point precisely. But I think you can answer that question yourself. Suppose now, my sister, that you wake up some bright morning holding precisely the same views respecting admission to the Lord's table that you now hold, but firmly convinced that immersion upon a public profession of faith in the Lord Jesus is the only scriptural baptism, and that sprinkling is not baptism at all, what would you be then? What could you be but a close communion Baptist?"

"Oh, I see it at last; I see it. Of course, I should be a Baptist, and that without changing my views about communion one bit. It is close baptism that makes it seem such close communion. How much I have wronged you Baptists by my hard thoughts and cruel words about your narrowness and bigotry; while it is all the while a noble, firm fidelity to principle. I hope you will forgive me, for I did it ignorantly, and rest assured I shall never again complain of close communion."

That good sister did not become a Baptist—being satisfied with her sprinkling—but she gave Baptists due credit for their integrity, in abiding the just consequences of their own convictions of Bible truth and Christian duty.

Happening in the city of X—— one day on business, and hearing a church bell, I dropped in, hoping to hear a sermon. I was not disappointed. The church was United Presbyterian, and the preacher (a wide-awake Scotchman) delivered an inspiring sermon. In it he discoursed of Christian charity. Alluding to the Baptists, and the abuse heaped upon them as close communionists, he said:

"The Baptists are no more chargeable with close communion than are the Presbyterians. They hold, in common with us, and, indeed, in common with the great body of evangelical Christians, that baptism is a scriptural prerequisite to the Lord's table. They are firmly convinced that immersion only is baptism; and therefore, as honest Christians, they can not invite to that table any who have not been immersed. All honor to the Baptists for their firm maintenance of principle in the face of bitter opposition. Let no man twit them of close communion. It is not a question about communion, but about baptism. We have no controversy with them about communion. It is a controversy about baptism, and about baptism only. We think they are wrong about baptism. Let us reason with them about that, and try to convince them that they are mistaken; but let us be honest and confess that if they are right about baptism, they are right about all the rest."

As I was an entire stranger to the congregation, and to the preacher, I knew that he had not said these things to flatter me, but because he was a well-informed, honest man, and loved to speak the truth.

In the beginning of my ministry, before I was ordained, I invited a Presbyterian minister to occupy my pulpit on communion Sabbath and administer the Lord's Supper, and he accepted my invitation.

There was at that time in my congregation a young man, a very recent convert, and a very zealous Christian worker. He was an Englishman, and had been sprinkled in infancy in the

Church of England. Afterward he had become an avowed atheist, and was such when I first met him. At his earnest request, I privately canvassed the whole ground of speculative atheism with him. I found him a sharp, trained reasoner, of a very decided metaphysical cast of mind, and our discussions were continued for several months. At length he was thoroughly convinced of his mistake, made a public renunciation of his atheism, sought Christ, and became a very devout, earnest Christian. His talents made him very useful, and he was almost immediately made superintendent of the Sunday-school, in which position he was doing good service at the time Rev. Mr. S—— came at my invitation to administer the Lord's Supper in my church. He had not united with any church, being in doubt about which one he ought to unite with. Ultimately he became a Congregationalist, and is now, and has been for many years, an honored and useful minister of the gospel in that denomination.

I loved him tenderly as a Christian brother, and a very dear friend, and, in common with many of my brethren, I greatly desired to have him sit down with us at the Lord's table. At that time I had not examined the question of communion, but was governed in the matter by misguided feelings, and consequently was in favor of open communion. So I spoke to Rev. Mr. S——, confidentially, and requested him to speak to Bro. H—— privately, and invite him to come to the table with us. I told of his recent conversion, his zeal for Christ, and our great love for him as a true and devoted disciple.

Mr. S—— listened attentively until I concluded, then he said:

"Is Bro. H—— a member of any church?"

"No; he has not yet decided where he ought to unite. He has that matter now under prayerful consideration."

"Well, I can not invite him to the Lord's table. That is an ordinance of the Church, and only those who are church-members have a right to come to it."

"Oh, but he is such a good man! We all love him so much! Do, please, invite him."

"No; I can not. As for loving him, you can love him just as well, and fellowship him just as much if he does not come to the table. The Lord's table is not to exhibit our love and fellowship for each other, but to commemorate the death of our Lord. It will be time enough for Bro. H—— to engage in the observance of this church service when he has become a member of the church."

"But Bro. H—— has been baptized; he was baptized in infancy in the Church of England. Isn't that enough?"

"No, sir. The Supper is a church ordinance, and it belongs, not to all who are baptized, but only to those who are baptized members of the church. Bro. H—— has been baptized, but he is not a member of any church. He was baptized by a minister of the Church of England. Very well. We respect his baptism. But he was not received into the membership of the Church of England. And he does not consider himself a member of that church, or of any other, and therefore he has no right at the Lord's table, and we have no right to invite him there until he unites with some evangelical church."

And Mr. S—— was firm, and I was obliged to submit to what I then deemed a very great hardship, and a grievous wrong. But I have long since learned that he was right in putting the order of the Lord's house above the clamor of private affection, or personal interest and feeling.

In refusing to invite Bro. H—— to the Lord's table he acted upon strict Presbyterian principles, and upon strict Baptist principles as well. And in support of his action, he might have arrayed the standard writers and authorities of almost every denomination in Christendom. Take a few samples. Dr. Doddridge, Congregationalist, says: "It is certain that, as far as our knowledge of antiquity reaches, no unbaptized person received the Lord's Supper." (*Lectures*, page 511.)

"How excellent soever any man's character is, he must be baptized before he can be looked upon as completely a member of the Church of Christ." (*Lectures*, page 511.)

Richard Baxter, Congregationalist, says: "What man dare go in a way that hath neither precept nor example to warrant it, from a way that hath a full current of both; yet they that will admit members into the visible church without baptism do so." (*Plain Scriptural Proof*, page 24.)

Rev. Dr. Dwight, Congregationalist, says: "*It is an indispensable qualification* for this ordinance that the candidate for communion be a member of the visible Church of Christ, in full standing. By this I intend that he should be a man of piety; that he should have made a public profession of religion, and that he should have been baptized." (*Systematic Theology*, Ser. 160.) Again he says (Ser. 156): "Except a man be born of water, and of the Spirit, etc. To be born of water is to be baptized. To be born of the Spirit is to be regenerated. The kingdom of God is a phrase used in the gospel in a twofold sense, and denotes his visible and invisible kingdom, or the collection of apparent and the collection of real saints. The indispensable condition of entering the former, or visible kingdom, is here made by our Savior, baptism. The indispensable qualification for admission into the invisible kingdom is regeneration, the great act of the Spirit of God, which constitutes men real saints. *Baptism, therefore, is here made, by Christ, a condition absolute to our authorized entrance into his visible Church.*"

Rev. Dr. Hopkins, Congregationalist, says: "No one is to be considered and treated as a member of the Church of Christ unless he be baptized with water, as this is the only door by which persons can be introduced into the visible kingdom of Christ, according to his appointment." (*Curtiss on Com.*, page 125.)

Rev. F. G. Hibbard, Methodist Episcopal, says (*Christian Baptism*, page 174, Second Part): "Before entering upon the argument before us, it is but just to remark that, in one principle, the Baptist and pedobaptist churches agree. They both agree in rejecting from the communion at the table of the Lord, and in denying the rights of church-fellowship to all who have not been baptized. Valid baptism, they consider, is essential to constitute visible church-membership. This also we hold. The only question, then, that here divides us is, What is essential to valid baptism? The Baptists, in passing the sweeping sentence of disfranchisement upon all other Christian churches, have only acted upon a principle held in common with all other Christian churches, viz.: that baptism is essential to church membership. They have denied our baptism, and, as unbaptized persons, we have been excluded from their table. That they err greatly in their views of Christian baptism we, of course, believe. But, according to their views of baptism, they certainly are consistent in restricting thus their communion. We would not be understood as passing a judgment of approval upon their course, but we say their views of baptism force them upon the ground of strict communion, and herein they act upon the same principles as other churches, *i. e.*, they admit only those whom they deem baptized persons to the communion table. Of course, they must be their own judges of what baptism is. It is evident that, according to our views of baptism, we can admit them to our communion; but with their views of baptism, it is equally evident that they can never reciprocate the courtesy. And the charge of close communion is no more applicable to the Baptists than to us, inasmuch as the question of church-fellowship with them is determined by as liberal principles as it is with any other Protestant churches, so far, I mean, as the present subject is concerned; *i. e., it is determined by valid baptism.*"

Dr. Wall, Episcopal, says (*Hist. Infant Baptism, Part II., Chap.* 9): "No church ever gave the communion to any persons before they were baptized. Among all the absurdities that ever were held, none ever maintained that any person should partake of the communion before he was baptized."

Open communion is a modern innovation, having no sanction in Scripture, in the history of the churches, or in reason.

That it has made some inroads upon the order and stability of some churches is readily conceded, and that it is a growing sentiment in many quarters is doubtless true; and yet the great body of Christian churches still reject it, and hold, with the much maligned Baptists, that baptism and church-membership are essential to an orderly participation in the solemn service of the Lord's Supper.

Even our Episcopal Methodist friends, although they invite all who, in their own judgment, are Christians, still testify in their Book of Discipline that they will admit no one to the Lord's table among them who is guilty of any practice for which they would exclude a member —a declaration in itself very wise and proper, but involving fully the principle of church control over the Table. Few Methodists will care to affirm that their church would not exclude from her membership any person who might actively denounce her doctrines as untrue, or her practices as unscriptural. If, for example, a member of that church should actively teach that the doctrine of the Church is false in respect to falling from grace, he would speedily be excluded. Or if he should teach vigorously that sprinkling and infant baptism are unscriptural and wrong, that they are inventions of men and ought to be put away as no baptism at all, and that all his brethren who are not immersed on a profession of faith are unbaptized, he would be promptly expelled from the church. And yet in all that he would be doing just what honest Baptists are doing all the time. And the Methodist Episcopal Church says, in an official way, in her Discipline, that she will admit no one to the Lord's table who is guilty of any practice for which she would exclude one of her own members. I submit, therefore, with all due deference, that the Methodist Episcopal Church is a close communion Church. If you say she is open communion, I admit it. The fact is, judged by her own official standards, she is both close communion and open communion, having *close communion principles, but open communion practices.*

Open communion is a modern thing altogether, without warrant in the word of God. There is not one solitary example or precept for it in the Scriptures. They are entirely silent about it—as a thing never heard of in that age. And the early history of the Church gives it no support. On the contrary, the explicit testimony of Justin Martyr, about the middle of the second century, shows that only baptized believers were then permitted to partake of the sacred Supper. He says, speaking of the Lord's Supper: "This food is called Eucharist, of which it is lawful for no other person to partake than one who believes what we teach to be true, and who has been bathed in the bath for the remission of sins, and unto regeneration, and who so lives, as Christ enjoins."

The catechism of the Church in Geneva, written by Calvin, embodies the universal view and practice of all churches, from the apostolic age to very recent times, with reference to the relation of baptism and the Supper. It says: "Is it enough to receive both (the sacraments) once in a lifetime?" "It is enough so to receive baptism, which may not be repeated. It is different with the Supper." "What is the difference?" "By baptism the Lord adopts us, and brings us into his Church, so as thereafter to regard us as a part of his household. After he has admitted us among the number of his people, he testifies by the Supper that he takes a continual interest in nourishing us."

Open communion has no support from sound reason. The Lord's Supper is intended to commemorate his death, not to manifest our Christian fellowship one with another. "For as often as ye eat this bread, and drink this cup, ye proclaim the Lord's death till he come." And Christ himself says, "This do in remembrance of me."

But suppose we grant for a moment all that the advocates of open communion claim, viz.: that the Supper is an act of Christian fellowship, *i. e.*, that in eating the Supper together, Christians express their fellowship one with another as Christians. It follows that each one who eats at that table thereby indorses all the rest who eat with him as Christians, for an act expressive of Christian fellowship for a person means an indorsement of that person as a Christian.

Are such indorsements to be given by Christian people carelessly? Are they to be scattered about promiscuously? Are they to be handed out generously to all who come along? Is there no responsibility incurred by an indiscriminate Christian fellowship? What would we think of a business man who would continually give certificates of character and financial responsibility to every man who would apply, on the mere affirmation of the applicant, that he was honest and responsible? Would we regard him as discreet? Would we deem him a safe and prudent man? Would we regard his certificates as valuable evidences of character and financial standing? No; we would think such a procedure either very wicked, or very foolish, or both— and very justly, too. And we would laugh at such certificates until the meanest beggar would be ashamed to take one. And yet our open communion friends, on their own showing, are scattering broadcast their certificates of Christian character quite as recklessly. They fellowship all who come, and invite all to come who desire to—putting the sacred Supper out in the street practically, at the mercy of every mendacious **tramp.** And then, when the motley crowd of good, bad and indifferent are gathered about, they proceed to express Christian fellowship with them, without the slightest evidence that they are all Christians. Is that wise? Is it prudent? Is it honorable? Is it reasonable? Look over the company of communicants. Yonder are half a dozen strangers. No one knows them. They may be good Christians, but they bring no evidence of it. For aught any one knows, they may be the basest of base hypocrites, yet a whole church proceeds to fellowship them as Christians. Can anything be more unreasonable? If those strangers eat and drink unworthily, and therefore to their own condemnation, they can justly plead that the church tempted them. If they prove utterly unworthy of confidence, there is no redress for the community or the church. They can present themselves at the Lord's table at the next communion season, and receive the full Christian fellowship of the very church whose confidence they have grossly abused; and, on open communion principles, there is no help for it. Is that reasonable?

But this is not the worst of it. Open communion practices break down all barriers and neutralize all church discipline. A member of the church proves himself a very bad man. The church promptly expels him from her membership—publicly withdraws the hand of fellowship, but at the next communion season that bad man presents himself at the Lord's table, in that same church, and the whole church expresses its Christian fellowship with him by eating and drinking with him. Is that reasonable? Does it tend to promote the purity of the church? Does it cultivate truthfulness and integrity in the church? Is it likely to make acts of discipline effective? And yet it is an inseparable part of the actual working of open communion.

If the act of partaking of the Lord's Supper is really expressive of Christian fellowship, then reason dictates the greatest caution in respect to our associates at the sacred table, lest we express Christian fellowship for those who are not Christians, and so bring reproach on the name of Christ.

More, real Christian fellowship can not exist in the absence of evidence of Christian character. In law, a man is deemed innocent until proven guilty, and in business a man is esteemed honest (yet with great caution) until proven dishonest. But in religion a man is not to be regarded as a Christian in the absence of satisfactory evidence. The mass of men are not Christians, and the drift of human nature is not in that direction. A stranger presents himself at the

Lord's table. That fact, of itself, does not establish his character as a Christian. For aught we know he may be a bad man. Certainly we do not know, with any reasonable degree of certainty, that he is a true Christian. How, then, can we honestly express Christian fellowship with him? We do not know his character, and therefore we do not and can not fellowship him as a Christian. If, then, we proceed to express Christian fellowship with him, we express that which does not exist, and our communion is the solemn enactment of a falsehood. If, then, the open communion view be the true one, and the act of eating the Lord's Supper with others is an expression of Christian fellowship with them, our only safety is to eat that Supper only with such persons as we thoroughly know and fully esteem as real Christians. For with such persons only can we have true, full Christian fellowship. It follows inevitably that our open communion friends are by their own principles reduced to this very remarkable dilemma—that they must choose between expressing a Christian fellowship which does not exist, or resort to the most rigid measures to restrict the expression of fellowship within due limits, so that the expression of fellowship shall not exceed the actual fellowship. But this compels a resort to the sternest sort of restricted communion as the only means of escape from bearing false witness at the table of our Lord. A system whose principles are so evidently, necessarily and fatally at war with its practices, can not be true.

The Scriptures plainly make baptism the first duty of the believer, whence it follows that it must precede the Supper. That is the order enjoined by our Lord (Matt. xxviii. 19, 20) in the great commission: "Go ye therefore, and teach all nations, baptizing them in the name of the Father, and of the Son, and of the Holy Ghost; teaching them to observe all things whatsoever I have commanded you." Teaching, baptizing, training—that is the divine order. And the inspired apostles so understood it, observing it in all their work. On the day of Pentecost they first preached the Word, then baptized those who believed, then broke bread. And this divine order is the sum total of close communion in Baptist Churches. Adherence to the law of Christ, as illustrated in the work of his apostles, is the head and front of our offending.

But what can we do about it? We must obey Christ and observe his ordinances as he instituted them, even though we be traduced for so doing. We are not separatists. We make no laws about either ordinance. We simply obey Christ. We want our brethren to do the same thing, and be one with us in doing as Christ directs. Isn't that fair? We ask no advantage, claim no superiority, assert no authority, but beg our brethren to obey our common Lord.

If they refuse to do it, and go off and set up other laws and contrary usages, we can not help it. We put up no bars, create no tests, and compel no divisions. Others go away and set up new tests, and establish new practices, and then ask us to put their new tests and new practices on a par with the old ones instituted by the Master; and because we can not do that, they call us hard names, brand us as bigots, and charge us with close communion. Is it bigotry to obey Christ? Is it wicked to observe his ordinances as he delivered them? Is it close communion to adhere to the order instituted by our Lord? Who are excluded by it? those who observe it? No! only those who prefer their own way to Christ's way. Our churches are open to all Christians who are willing to come into the Church in Christ's way. They can come in exactly as we did—in Christ's way. And the Lord's table among us is open to them on precisely the same terms as to ourselves; they can come to it in Christ's way just as freely as we can.

And yet they say we exclude them. It is a

mistake; they exclude themselves. We show them the law of Christ, and they refuse to obey it, and go off and set up for themselves. Is that our fault? Must we give up Christ's way, and adopt their way, to win them back? We could not succeed, if we were willing to try it. Somebody would invent some other new way, and many would accept it, and the divisions and discords would constantly multiply.

But we dare not do it. We must obey Christ, for he is King in Zion, and he alone. We love our brethren much, but we love Christ more. We dread their harsh, bitter, unjust words, for they hurt; but we dread the displeasure of our King more. So we will keep on in the old paths, ever holding out the torch of truth, and the olive branch of peace, in the name of Christ.

NUMBER XIV.

"He that hath my commandments, and keepeth them, he it is that loveth me." . . . *"If a man love me, he will keep my words."* . . . *" Ye are my friends, if ye do whatsoever I command you."* . . . *"He that loveth me not, keepeth not my sayings."*—*Jesus.*

WITH these tender but decisive words of the Master before me, I could not do less than test my pedobaptist practices by his words.

Doing that as fairly and as impartially as I could, I was obliged to give them up, as opposed to his commandments, contrary to his example, and subversive of his life-giving words. This was not an easy thing for me to do, for I loved my pedobaptist brethren very dearly, and my love was evidently reciprocated by them; but when the crucial test came, my sorrowing heart was made glad by the discovery that, much as I loved them, I loved the Master more. I make no boast; only by grace I am what I am. If I braved loss for his sake, it was because his love impelled me. If I attained to definite and firm convictions of scriptural truth, it is because his words are definite and firm, and easily understood by the earnest and prayerful seeker after truth. But I was not alone in these things. In those dark and trying hours there was one by my side who is yet the light and solace of my life, who, by her faith in God, her love of Christ, and her keen, intuitive perceptions of his truth, was to me a tower of strength—my quiet, retiring, but resolute and self-sacrificing wife, whose heroic counsel has ever been, *Dare to do right, no matter what it may cost.*

These sketches are, as their title imports, from real life. There is neither fancy nor fiction about them. The incidents narrated and the conversations detailed actually occurred. "With malice toward none," but "charity toward all," I have herein related a few of the many things entering into my experiences in the study of baptism, in the hope that the relation may prove serviceable to those who desire to know and do the truth, suppressing only the names of my interlocutors, to whom I would not knowingly do aught of harm. They are brethren of many noble qualities. Some of them have entered into their rest, while others still labor in hope, earnestly looking forward to refreshment and reward. With their virtues and graces I have no controversy; I combat only their errors. As noble men I revere them; as Christians I love them; as errorists I oppose them. I honor their virtues, emulate their graces, and seek to correct their errors. Nor do I, in this, pretend that I am infallible, or free from error. "To err is human," and many years of close observation have taught me that he is doomed to disappointment who seeks perfection beneath the stars. But of all types of imperfection, that is the most censurable which is content with itself, and cherishes its own errors, or the errors of others, excusing itself because no mortal, with undimmed eye, discerns perfectly all parts of the absolute truth.

Grant that I am in error in many things, as almost certainly I am; then let those who perceive my errors teach me the truth, and as they verify it by the divine Word, I will gladly receive it, and thank them for their kind offices. It is in this spirit that I have written these sketches. I love my pedobaptist brethren as Christian brethren—Christian and beloved—but in error in a matter of vast importance, and far-reaching in its consequences. I believe they love the truth, and I would help them to perceive it by clearing away some, at least, of the fogs error has exhaled about it. Immersion of adults is as impotent to make men Christians as is the sprinkling of infants; but immersion is a duty enjoined by our Lord himself upon those who believe in him, while sprinkling—infant and adult—is an invention of men which actually obscures many portions of the divine Word, and in the case of millions prevents obedience to the plain commandment of Christ.

I do not say, I dare not say, that immersion is essential to salvation; but I do say, on the authority of the Lord himself, that obedience to his commandments, at least so far as the import of those commandments can be perceived, is indispensable to honest, genuine discipleship, and that he only who is willing to render prompt and cheerful obedience to the words of Christ in all things, so far as their meaning can be discovered, is entitled to call himself a Christian, or to demand recognition of his Christian character from others.

I am not a Baptist because I love much water rather than little, but because Jesus commands immersion instead of sprinkling, and the immersion of those who believe instead of unconscious babes, and his commandments are the supreme law of my life. With me it is not a question of water, nor a question of getting to heaven, but a question of *loyalty to Christ* and of *fitness for heaven*, and in this I do not differ from the great mass of my Baptist brethren everywhere.

If any one says, "It is a matter of indifferency, since we can get to heaven without scriptural baptism," I reply: Is the desire and will of your Master of so little consequence to you? Do you not care whether you obey him or not? If you do not, then I fear you love him not, since he says: "If a man love me, he will keep my words."

Rest assured, if you do not care to obey Christ, you really do not love him, since he says: "He that loveth me not keepeth not my sayings." Does that describe you? If so, heaven would prove but an irksome prison, should you chance somehow to get there. Beware! there is danger in such indifferency.

But I am confident there are many thousands of pedobaptists who honestly and earnestly desire to know the truth about these matters, and who will gladly welcome aid, no matter whence it may come, if only it contributes to open to them the temple of truth.

To such I send forth these brief sketches, with an earnest prayer that their mission of love may not prove fruitless.

And if, by and by, I am permitted to know that they have been of use in guiding earnest souls into the light, and in leading them to put away the inventions of men, and to cherish and observe the ordinances of Christ in their simplicity and purity, I will rejoice that I have not suffered and studied and written in vain.

And may grace, mercy and peace, from God the Father and Christ Jesus our Lord, rest upon all readers of these sketches for the Master's sake.

THE END.

WHAT THE PAPERS SAY

OF

Behind the Scenes.

IF any of our readers want a book that if read, will stiffen their backbone as Baptists, let them send to the JOURNAL AND MESSENGER, Cincinnati, O., and ask for "Behind the Scenes." We read the articles as they were printed in the columns of that paper, and pronounce them among the best things of the kind we ever read. — *Baptist Nation.*

WE have just received the book, and regard it as among the most interesting additions made to our literature on the baptismal question in half a dozen years. It will be interesting reading to Baptists and pedobaptists as well. We commend it heartily. —*Alabama Baptist.*

THE arguments are extremely telling and cogent, yet they are urged in a kind, Christian, not in the least bitter spirit. —*Christian Secretary.*

NO one can fail to be benefited by reading carefully this unique book. Pedobaptists will find themselves fairly represented, and their views in general correctly stated. —*Texas Baptist.*

WE congratulate the author and thank the publisher, and commend the volume to all our readers. It is the very book to put into the hands of inquiring pedobaptists. Send and get it. —*Arkansas Evangelist.*

AS we said a few weeks ago, it is a book that will do to buy, to read and to lend. — *Texas Baptist Herald.*

THESE sketches as they appeared in the JOURNAL AND MESSENGER attracted wide attention. In the permanent form in which they now appear, they are worthy of the widest circulation. —*Zion's Advocate.*

IT is the very book for the masses of the people and for Baptists to loan to their pedobaptist neighbors and relatives. — *Tennessee Baptist*

THE book is not only interesting but very instructive, and should be read by old and young. —*Biblical Recorder.*

THE book ought to be in every Baptist family, and it is an excellent thing to put into the hands of any who desire to know about the Baptists. We give it hearty commendation. —*Central Baptist.*

NO recent contribution to Baptist literature has been more gladly welcomed. —*Michigan Christian Herald.*

WE are pained to know that Mr. Iams charges pedobaptists with lack of candor, but it is more painful to observe that he has proved his case. —*Watchman.*

THE book has not a dull page in it, and is not only exceedingly interesting as a narrative, but can not but prove helpful to earnest, inquiring minds who desire to know and do their duty. —*Baptist Weekly.*

IT is not often that a book deserves to be read at once as this does by everybody, and especially by every pedobaptist. It tells the story of the baptismal controversy capitally. The little book will make an impression and rank first class in polemic literature. —*Herald of Truth.*

WE trust the book may accomplish great good in opening the eyes of our pedobaptist friends to the weakness and unscripturalness of their position, and that they may have not only light to see, but grace to follow the right. — *National Baptist.*

THE story is a captivating one; is bestudded at every point with sparkling gems of truth, and is so presented as to disarm prejudice at the outset. We know of no book so valuable as a hand-book for Baptists to use with their pedobaptist friends. Send and get the book and loan it, and keep on loaning it. —*American Baptist Reflector.*

WE emphatically commend the book. Our brethren in the ministry of other denominations ought to read it. —*Watch Tower.*

THE sketches are well written, very sensible and pointed, and show very conclusively the inconsistencies of pedobaptists, and the logical correctness of Baptist views, as well as their accordance with Scripture. The book is not only interesting but very instructive, and should be read by old and young. —*Kind Words.*

WE had one chapter of its contents in the MESSENGER a few weeks since, and may possibly extract another shortly, but the book should be read to be fully appreciated. — *Christian Messenger, Halifax, Nova Soctia.*

THERE is no dullness, nor sameness, nor weariness going over old ground, in a single page. It is bright, spicy, eloquent, amusing, instructive, with a frank, manly, Pauline piety and devotion to truth which can not fail to promt every reader......

This book is so well and wittily written that it would interest a man who cared nothing for Christ's commands. It is, of all books on the subject we have seen, the best for Baptists to put into the hands of pedobaptist friends; the New Testament, of course, excepted. It is the very thing for the young Baptists to read on this subject, and it will be a treat to older Baptists who have grown a little weary of the usual style of such books. —*Western Recorder.*

A Biographical Sketch of Francis Marion Iams (1830-1892)

By
John Franklin Jones

A Biographical Sketch of Francis Marion Iams (1830-1892)

Francis Marion Iams (Ijames, Imes) was born 27 July 1830 in Licking County, Monroe Township, Ohio. He was the fifth of eight children born to William M. Ijams (ca. 1800-1863) and Mariah Jane Bailey Ijams (ca. 1804-1849) (Reynolds). He spent his youth on a farm in Delaware County, Ohio (*Banner*).

At various times in his life, Iams worked as a farmer, an educator, a Congregational minister, a frontier missionary, and a Baptist minister. He lived at various times in several states. His known residences in chronological order include the following states and localities: Ohio (Monroe and Delaware counties); Illinois (McHenry County, and Leroy); Wisconson (Reedsburg, Tomah, and Menominee County); Ohio (Mt. Vernon); Kansas (Parsons and Salina); Ohio (Mt. Vernon; Mansfield; and Copopa); Michigan (Leslie); and Ohio (Mt. Vernon).

The 1860 US Census provided the first extant record of Francis' religious life. The record listed him as a Congregational clergyman (1860 US Census). He was ordained a Congregational minister in April 1860 and served as such until 1866 (*Banner*). The particular early religious influences upon him, the circumstances of his conversion, his specific church affiliation/s, his call and surrender to preach, any formal education, and the Congregational churches he served have not yet come to light.

JOHN FRANKLIN JONES

More, however, is known about the Baptist churches he served. He was pastor of the Mt. Vernon Baptist Church, Mt. Vernon, Ohio (1875-1878); the First Baptist Church, Parsons, Kansas (1879); the Mansfield Baptist Church, Mansfield Ohio (1881-1885); the Columbia Baptist Church, Copopa, Ohio (1888-?), and at Leslie, Michigan (*Banner*).

During his tenure in Kansas, Iams received support from the American Baptist Home Mission Society as a home missionary. Records indicate that missionary affiliation while at Parsons, Kansas (for nine months) (FBC) and Salina, Kansas (for seven months) in 1879-1880 (Layton).

Iams was active in his local community. Local records indicate that he performed many weddings. He united with other citizens in opposing activities which he felt to be harmful to the community's moral tone. He regularly participated in the associations of churches and in his state and national conventions. He actively promoted Bible study and participated in the Sunday School movement.

Iams authored two books and some pamphlets: *Behind the Scenes: Sketches from Real life. By a Pastor.* [pseud.]. Cincinnati: George W. Lasher, 1883; *Before the Foot-lights.* Cincinnati, George W. Lasher, 1885; *Concessions of Pedobaptist Writers, As to the Subject and Mode of Baptism.* Cincinnati: George W. Lasher, n.d.; and *A Sober Inquiry, or, Christ's Reign with His Saints a Thousand Years* (N.p, n.d.) (Star).

He married Mary M. "Polly" Sanders (5 January 1833-22 December 1897) 3 March 1850 in McHenry County, Illinois. She was the daughter of Jacob and Hannah Sanders (Ross).

Iams and his wife parented seven children: Clayton M. (5 March 1851), Loretta Angelia (ca. 1853), Mary Angeline (14 May 1854), William "Willie" Henry (11 October 1856), Nellie Jane (29 December 1858), Charles Claude (23 October 1860), and Frank Curtis (16 May 1865). His son, Clayton M., was also a Baptist minister.

A Biographical Sketch of Francis Marion Iams

Iams died 17 June 1892 in Mount Vernon, Ohio (Knox County) and was buried in Mount View Cemetery, Knox County, Ohio (Richland).

BIBLIOGRAPHY

1850 US Census Illinois, Boone, Leroy, Roll: M432_98 page 73. Cited in Roberta Ross. Email to the writer, 11 August 2006 PM.

1860 US Census, Wisconsin, Monroe, Tomah page 191. Cited in Roberta Ross. Email to the writer, 11 August 2006 PM.

1880 US Census, Kansas, Salina. Cited in Carole Paprocki. Email to the writer, 23 August 2006, 11:16 PM.

1880 US Census, Knox Co., Ohio page 265B. Cited in Roberta Ross. Email to the writer, 11 August 2006 PM.

First Baptist Church of Parsons, Kansas. "Minutes of Business Meeting, 15 May 1879. Parsons, KA: First Baptist Church, 1897. Photocopied Cited as FBC.

http://archiver.rootsweb.com/th/read/WIWINNEB/2003-08/1061913388. Accessed 29 June 2006.

http://genforum.genealogy.com/iams/messages/44.html. Accessed 29 June 2006.

http://search.ancestry.com/cgi-bin/sse.dll?gl=allgs&gst=&rank=1&=%2c%2c%2c%2c%2c%2c%2c%2c%2c%2c%2c%2c%2c%2c%2c%2c%2c%2c&gsfn=f+m&gsln=iams&gsby=&gsb2co=2%2cUnited+States&gsb2pl=38%2cOhio&gsdy=&gsd2co=1%2cAll+Countries&gsd2pl=1%2c+&sbo=0&srchb=r&db=&ti=0&ti.si=0&gss=angs-b&ghc=50&fh=50&fsk=BEDpR60IgAAcqwfqYcI-61 -. Accessed 31 July 2006.

http://skyways.lib.ks.us/genweb/archives/labette/1901/321-334.shtml. Accessed 29 June 2006.

http://www.heritagepursuit.com/Knox/KnoxFile4.htm. Accessed 29 June 2006.

http://www.rootsweb.com/~ohrichla/MAR-1883.htm. Accessed 29 June 2006.

http://www.rootsweb.com/~ohrichla/MAR-1884.htm. Accessed 29 June 2006.

http://www.rootsweb.com/~ohrichla/MAR-1885.htm. Accessed 29 June 2006.

http://www.rootsweb.com/~ohrichla/Hist-JJ.htm. Accessed 29 June 2006.

Layton, Betty. E-mail to the writer, 23 August 2006. Cited as Layton.

Mansfield Baptist Association. *Minutes of the Sixty-second Anniversary of the Mansfield Baptist Association.* Loudonville, OH: Advocate Power Press, 1881.

Mansfield Baptist Association. *Minutes of the Sixty-fourth Anniversary of the Mansfield Baptist Association.* Gallion, OH: Inquirer Power Press, 1863.

The Mt. Vernon Baptist Association. *Minutes of the Thirty-fourth Anniversary of the Mt. Vernon Baptist Association...* Mt. Gilead, OH: N.p., 1876.

The Mt. Vernon Baptist Association. *Minutes of the Thirty-fifth Anniversary of the Mt. Vernon Baptist Association...* Mt. Gilead, OH: N.p., 1877.

The Mt. Vernon Baptist Association. *Minutes of the Thirty-sixth Anniversary of the Mt. Vernon Baptist Association...* Mt. Gilead, OH: N.p., 1878.

Mt. Vernon (OH) Democratic Banner. 23 June 1892. Cited in Carole Paprocki. Email to the writer, 23 August 2006, 11:16 PM. Cited as *Banner.*

Ohio Baptist Convention. *Proceedings of the Fifty-fifth Convention of the State of Ohio*. Granville, OH: Times Book & Job Printing House, 1880.

Ohio Baptist Convention. *Proceedings of the Sixty-third Anniversay of the Ohio Baptist Convention...* Norwalk, OH: Fair Publishing House, 1888.

Ohio Baptist Convention. *Proceedings of the Sixty-Seventh Anniversary of the Ohio Baptist Convention.* N.p; n.d., 40-42. Cited in Betty Layton. E-mail to the writer, 23 August 2006.

Paprocki, Carole. Email to the writer, 23 August 2006, 11:16 PM. Cited as Paprocki.

Richland Co., Ohio Genealogical Society. Cited in Roberta Ross. Email to the writer, 11 August 2006.

Reynolds, Ralph D. *Iams of America: Landed Gentry of Maryland Patriots, Pioneers, and Successful Americans.* Masthof Press, 1998 Softcover. ISBN:1-883294-63-0 / 1883294630. Cited in Roberta Ross. Email to the writer, 11 August 2006.

Ross, Roberta. Email to the writer, 11 August 2006. Cited as Ross.

Starr, Edward C., ed., *A Baptist Bibliography Being a Register of Printed Material By and About Baptists; Including Works Written Against the Baptists.* 24 vols. Chester, PN: American Baptist Historical Society, 1953. S.v. "Iams, F. M."

Sister, B. and B., eds. *Early West Tennessee Marriages,* Vol. 2. Nashville, TN: N.p., n.d. Cited in Roberta Ross. Email to the writer, 11 August 2006.

BY JOHN FRANKLIN JONES
Cordova, Tennessee
August 2006

THE BAPTIST STANDARD BEARER, INC.

a non-profit, tax-exempt corporation
committed to the Publication & Preservation
of the Baptist Heritage.

CURRENT TITLES AVAILABLE IN
THE BAPTIST *DISTINCTIVES* SERIES

KIFFIN, WILLIAM   A Sober Discourse of Right to Church-Communion. Wherein is proved by Scripture, the Example of the Primitive Times, and the Practice of All that have Professed the Christian Religion: That no Unbaptized person may be Regularly admitted to the Lord's Supper. (London: George Larkin, 1681).

KINGHORN, JOSEPH   Baptism, A Term of Communion. (Norwich: Bacon, Kinnebrook, and Co., 1816)

KINGHORN, JOSEPH   A Defense of "Baptism, A Term of Communion". In Answer To Robert Hall's Reply. (Norwich: Wilkin and Youngman, 1820).

GILL, JOHN   Gospel Baptism. A Collection of Sermons, Tracts, etc., on Scriptural Authority, the Nature of the New Testament Church and the Ordinance of Baptism by John Gill. (Paris, AR: The Baptist Standard Bearer, Inc., 2006).

CARSON, ALEXANDER	Ecclesiastical Polity of the New Testament. (Dublin: William Carson, 1856).
BOOTH, ABRAHAM	A Defense of the Baptists. A Declaration and Vindication of Three Historically Distinctive Baptist Principles. Compiled and Set Forth in the Republication of Three Books. Revised edition. (Paris, AR: The Baptist Standard Bearer, Inc., 2006).
BOOTH, ABRAHAM	Paedobaptism Examined on the Principles, Concessions, and Reasonings of the Most Learned Paedobaptists. With Replies to the Arguments and Objections of Dr. Williams and Mr. Peter Edwards. 3 volumes. (London: Ebenezer Palmer, 1829).
CARROLL, B. H.	*Ecclesia* - The Church. With an Appendix. (Louisville: Baptist Book Concern, 1903).
CHRISTIAN, JOHN T.	Immersion, The Act of Christian Baptism. (Louisville: Baptist Book Concern, 1891).
FROST, J. M.	Pedobaptism: Is It From Heaven Or Of Men? (Philadelphia: American Baptist Publication Society, 1875).
FULLER, RICHARD	Baptism, and the Terms of Communion; An Argument. (Charleston, SC: Southern Baptist Publication Society, 1854).
GRAVES, J. R.	Tri-Lemma: or, Death By Three Horns. The Presbyterian General Assembly Not Able To Decide This Question: "Is Baptism In The Romish Church Valid?" 1st Edition.

	(Nashville: Southwestern Publishing House, 1861).
MELL, P.H.	Baptism In Its Mode and Subjects. (Charleston, SC: Southern Baptist Publications Society, 1853).
JETER, JEREMIAH B.	Baptist Principles Reset. Consisting of Articles on Distinctive Baptist Principles by Various Authors. With an Appendix. (Richmond: The Religious Herald Co., 1902).
PENDLETON, J.M.	Distinctive Principles of Baptists. (Philadelphia: American Baptist Publication Society, 1882).
THOMAS, JESSE B.	The Church and the Kingdom. A New Testament Study. (Louisville: Baptist Book Concern, 1914).
WALLER, JOHN L.	Open Communion Shown to be Unscriptural & Deleterious. With an introductory essay by Dr. D. R. Campbell and an Appendix. (Louisville: Baptist Book Concern, 1859).

For a complete list of current authors/titles, visit our internet site at:
www.standardbearer.org
or write us at:

he Baptist Standard Bearer, Inc.

NUMBER ONE IRON OAKS DRIVE • PARIS, ARKANSAS 72855
TEL # 479-963-3831   *FAX # 479-963-8083*
EMAIL: Baptist@centurytel.net   *http://www.standardbearer.org*

Thou hast given a standard to them that fear thee; that it may be displayed because of the truth. — Psalm 60:4

www.ingramcontent.com/pod-product-compliance
Lightning Source LLC
Chambersburg PA
CBHW020752160426
43192CB00006B/320